TOLD IN THE HUTS

THE Y.M.C.A GIFT BOOK

Y.M.C.A

Contributed by Soldiers & War Workers.
With Introduction by Arthur K. Yapp.

Illustrated by the late Cyrus Cuneo, being the last work of this famous Artist

Published for the Benefit of the Y.M.C.A. Active Service Campaign amongst our Soldiers, Sailors & Munition Workers, in all parts of the World.

LONDON.
JARROLD & SONS

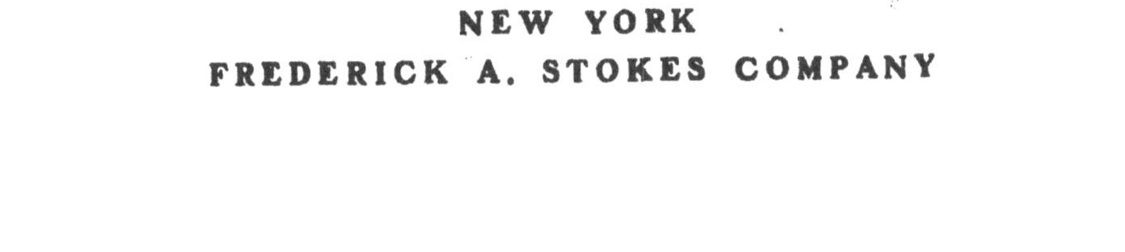

NEW YORK
FREDERICK A. STOKES COMPANY

THE GREAT SEA BATTLE.

By
Gracious Permission
this Book
is dedicated to
Her Majesty Queen Alexandra

Cumberland Lodge
1916

To my fellow workers in the Y.M.C.A. send the following Christmas message.

"Tho' the seasons are full of changes
And the old gives place to the new,
Yet I send you the same sweet message
From a heart that is warm & true.
I know that the old time greeting
Is the best I can wish for you. —
                            E.H.S."

Victoria
Princess of Schleswig Holstein
        President of Ladies Aux. Comttee
                            Y.M.C.A.

TARBAT HOUSE,
KILDARY,
ROSS-SHIRE.

It is with very great pleasure that I send all the readers of this Gift Book my best wishes for a Happy Christmas and for Peace in the coming year.

Both Sir John and myself have been very interested in all the War work carried out so well by the Y.M.C.A., and trust that their further efforts will be crowned with continued success.

Gwendoline Jellicoe

ABERDOUR HOUSE,
ABERDOUR,
FIFE

  We are now at the beginning of the third year of the great War. The struggle & sacrifice has been very great, not only for those who are taking an active part, our Sailors & Soldiers - but also for the silent ones at home, who are working day & night, & are helping on the end - the Victorious End.

  The Y.M.C.A. is doing a very big share in this work, & I am sure we all wish it success.

      Yours sincerely

      Ethel Beatty

Contents.

		PAGE
DEDICATION TO H.M. QUEEN ALEXANDRA		1
WISHES FROM PRINCESS VICTORIA (facsimile)		2
LADY JELLICOE'S LETTER (facsimile)		3
LADY BEATTY'S LETTER (facsimile)		4
INTRODUCTION	Arthur K. Yapp	7
APPRECIATION FROM GENERAL BIRDWOOD		11
WHAT IT IS LIKE AT THE FRONT	Sir R. Baden-Powell	15
SWEET LAVENDER	Geo. A. Birmingham	19
THE END OF THE DREAM	Geo. Goodchild	25
PRO PATRIA	Rev. John Safeley, M.A.	31
A PACKET OF WOODBINES	Paul Trent	33
MY LAND	Betty Dundas	36
THE ADVANCE	Levorno Sabatini	37
"IT WAS ME, SARGINT!"	One of the Third Line	41
A BIT OF BUNTING	By a Wounded Anzac	45
BEHIND THE LINES	The Hon. Mrs. Stuart Wortley	48
AN EXCHANGE OF FAVOURS	Eric De Banzie	53
THE V.C. PADRE	A. Gordon Hamlin	56
TEN DAYS	Pte. J. C., K.R.R.	59
THE GHASTLY EXPERIENCE OF A 2ND LIEUTENANT	Capt. H. Harrop	64
"RICKETY BILL"	Joseph Hocking	69
KEEP YOUR HEAD WELL DOWN	By a Sergeant, R.F.	74
A NOVICE IN A SUBMARINE	E. Allison Burrows	75
WENDERSBY THE "IMMORTAL"	Bomb. G. H., R.G.A.	79
THE PHANTOM 'PLANE	Levorno Sabatini	85
SLEEP WELL	Miss N. L. Eley	89
PEACE DAY	W. Pett Ridge	91
THE "FORTY-NINE"	Pte. A. H., H.A.C.	95
THE SEVEN WONDERS OF THE Y.M.C.A. HUT WORLD	Arthur K. Yapp	101
THE ATHEIST	Geo. Goodchild	105
THE RED CROSS AND THE RED TRIANGLE	Lady Rodney	120
YOUR KING AND COUNTRY NEED YOU	———	123
HOW SERGEANT JUBY WON THE D.C.M.	Levorno Sabatini	127
IN A GARRISON TOWN	———	130
HOME ON LEAVE	"Ian Hay."	133

Contents.

		PAGE
THE KEY TO THE DOOR	Annie S. Swan	135
THE PICKET PATROL	Gunner L. T., R.G.A.	141
CONCERTS AT THE FRONT	Miss Lena Ashwell	147
ADVENTURES ON THE PENINSULA	By a Y.M.C.A. Leader	151
COMRADESHIP	Right Hon. G. W. E. Russell	157
"EARWIG"	Rifleman X., R.B.	161
THE BRAVERY OF WOMEN	———	166
"COOK'S MATE"	Gunner L. T., R.G.A.	169
ON THE WAY BACK	A. St. John Adcock	173
"LITTLE TOOTS"	———	177
THE "NIGHT HAWKS"	Levorno Sabatini	181
A "QUIET" DAY IN ANZAC REGION	Corpl. J. Doggett, Australian Imp. Force	193
TRUE TILL DEATH	———	200
THE PHILOSOPHY OF SWEARING	E. G. Miles	203
THE SHELL HOLE	———	209
WAS IT SUPERSTITION?	Basil Yeaxlee	214
THREE BOYS IN KHAKI	———	217
ADDING INSULT TO INJURY	———	221
Y.M.C.A. MEN WHO HAVE WON THE V.C.	Basil Yeaxlee	223
THE PRODIGAL	———	228
"THE WOWSER"	———	229
"SMUGGY"	———	231
"BE BRITISH—KEEP OFF"	A. K. Y.	235
THE STORY OF AN AMBUSCADE	A. K. Y.	236

Illustrations.

THE GREAT SEA BATTLE	Cyrus Cuneo	Frontispiece
THE POPULAR RENDEZVOUS FOR SOLDIERS IN LONDON		facing page 12
WE ARE DOWN-HEARTED, I DON'T THINK!	Sir R. Baden-Powell	,, 15
THEY BOMBED THEIR WAY UP THE ENEMY TRENCH		,, 37
FOUR SKETCHES	Bert Wardle	58, 220
REPULSING A FRONTAL ATTACK	Cyrus Cuneo	,, 68
THE ENEMY CRASHED TO THE EARTH	Cyrus Cuneo	,, 100
THE CRIMEAN VETERAN	Bert Wardle	,, 123
A THRILLING CHARGE	Cyrus Cuneo	,, 133
THE GREAT PUSH	Bert Wardle	,, 147
SOUVENIR HUNTERS	Pte. MacMichael	,, 181
REPRODUCTION OF TRENCH MAGAZINE, "THE GASPER"		189-192
LANDING AT GALLIPOLI	Cyrus Cuneo	,, 197
AND ABOUT 150 MARGINAL SKETCHES		

Introduction.

By Arthur K. Yapp.

OH! that the Huts could speak! What tales they would have to tell! Huts that are not huts! Huts that are mere stables or farm outbuildings! Huts that are palatial establishments catering for the needs of thousands of men! The little brown Hut made of timber, and roofed with felt, serving the men at outposts in the danger zone of the East Coast—on the wilds of Salisbury Plain—dotted about in hundreds of camps in all parts of the United Kingdom!

What a romantic story could be told by the dug-out Hut at Anzac! What did the Turks do with it when our men evacuated the Peninsula? Or the Huts that are as busy as beehives on the banks of the Tigris, in the wilds of British or German East Africa, or on either bank of the Suez Canal! What stories they could tell!

Then there are the Huts in France. One wishes those in the great Base Camps could tell their story of men heartened by the touch they have given them of home life when far away from home; of the splendid concerts and cinema entertainments; crowded meetings when men have felt themselves stirred to the depths at the Old, Old Story that has been told in all its simplicity, but with persuasive earnestness that has carried conviction, and has helped them to realise as they left the meetings to go " up the line " that they were not facing the ordeal of battle alone.

The Padre

Introduction.

The Hostel Huts, too, where the friends of dangerously wounded men are entertained by the Y.M.C.A. free of charge ! If they could tell what they have seen and heard, it would be one of the most human stories ever told—a story of broken hearts bound up by the loving hands of Christian sympathy and love.

And what of the Huts at the Fronts in France and Flanders ? The Y.M.C.A. Hut and the Y.M.C.A. man, both bearing the mystic sign of the Red Triangle, mean everything to the men in khaki in Flanders. The French people speak of the Y.M.C.A. as "Les Ygrec em ce ah," and will pass its red triangle anywhere. "Tommy Atkins" calls it "home," and to him it stands for all that is best and truest and noblest in "dear old Blighty," as he affectionately terms the land he loves "across the sea."

This book tells a few of the thousands of stories of reckless daring and deathless heroism that have been recounted from time to time in the Huts of the Y.M.C.A. It also recounts some of the more prosaic tales that our splendid men delight to tell one another in the Huts. The book has not been prepared with a view to "boosting" the Y.M.C.A., but incidentally it draws attention to one of the greatest social and religious movements of our time.

The Story of the Ploegsteert Hut.

When the Right Hon. Winston Spencer Churchill was in Flanders, he happened to be on duty with his men in the trenches on the ridge of Ploegsteert Wood. It was a Saturday night in early spring. All was quiet, and as "black as pitch." Shortly before midnight a star shell shot up from the German trenches and lit up the whole countryside with an unearthly brilliance. This was followed by others, and the effect was weird in the extreme. Presently the shriek

Tommy at Play

Introduction.

of a shell indicated that the enemy contemplated an attack. The shell burst in flames in front of the little Y.M.C.A. Hut. The noise of the explosion roused the workers in the Hut, and in less than four minutes they had slipped into their clothes and taken shelter in the dug-out which had been previously prepared fifteen yards to the rear of the building. They had only reached safety in the nick of time. A second shell burst inside the Hut, and the flames shot up sky-high, and for an hour and a half the Huns "strafed" the hill and wood for all they were worth, pouring in thousands of shells of every size and description. With the morning light not a vestige of the Hut was to be seen. A Y.M.C.A. worker, searching amidst the ruins, found the shrivelled-up rims of his eye-glasses, and a soldier hunting for souvenirs found two coins, a two-franc piece and a twenty-centime piece welded together by the heat. That was all that was left of the "home" the boys had loved for months past.

One striking incident of the night remains to be told. Whenever there came a moment's lull between the booming of the guns, nightingales sung in the Ploegsteert Wood as if nothing out of the common was taking place.

The Story of the Euston Hut.

The charming little Y.M.C.A. Hut that serves the men arriving at or departing from Euston Station was the first Hut with sleeping accommodation opened by the Y.M.C.A. in London during the War. In the early days as many as 420 men, passing through London on their way to or from the Front, have sought its friendly shelter on a single night.

Seven Scottish soldiers found their way in one morning. They were tired, home-sick, and depressed. Even a good square meal was not sufficient to revive their drooping spirits. They had said good-bye to their wives and bairns the day

Resting

Introduction.

before, and had travelled through the night in a crowded train, so that they had been unable to sleep a wink. They were on their way to the Dardanelles, and well they knew what they had to face. Chancing to look over the counter into the kitchen, one of the men—McTavish, we will call him—saw a lady worker shelling peas, and summoning all his courage—for these men, brave as they are, are very shy—asked if he might come and help her. Of course she welcomed him, and later on his six comrades came forward to assist in the operation. That morning they shelled enough peas to last a week. When they had completed the self-imposed task, McTavish spoke again: "I cannot tell ye the like of what that has meant to us. It has taken us right back home, and now we are ready to go to the Dardanelles or to face whatever the future may have in store."

A touch of home, that is what the men find in the Huts. There is nothing official about them, and the one commodity they do not possess is "red-tape." The boys yearn for home!

One day the Leader of the Euston Hut noticed a group of ragged children gathered outside the main entrance. He watched them as they approached nearer and nearer the door. Some of them summoned up their courage and walked right in as if they owned the whole place. This was too much for him. He went up to them and said, "You must run away; this place is not for boys and girls, it is for soldiers and sailors." One little ragged urchin looked up in his face and said, "Please, sir, we have given our money towards this show and we want to see how it is run." When he made enquiries he found that they belonged to one of the poorest of the schools in the North of London, and out of their poverty they had given no less than thirty shillings, nearly the whole of it in halfpennies and farthings, towards the cost of the work of the Y.M.C.A.

"Tommy's Home"

Appreciation from General Birdwood.

1st ANZAC CORPS, FRANCE,
September 19th, 1916.

DEAR SIR,

I understand that it is proposed to publish a "Gift Book" in the autumn for the benefit of the Y.M.C.A., and I write to send you my best wishes for the success of the book. I sincerely trust that it may prove of great advantage to the Society, which has done so much for the soldiers of our Empire since this war began.

I was fortunate enough to come in contact with the good work done by the Y.M.C.A. when the Australian and New Zealand Forces were concentrated in Egypt towards the end of 1914. Our troops were, of course, quite strange to that country, which generally makes settling down extremely difficult. We, however, found most willing help at hand immediately in the form of the Y.M.C.A., which at once came to our aid, and organised amusements, writing-rooms, tea-rooms, etc., for the Australian and New Zealand troops over a wide area of scattered camps, of which the men at once took grateful advantage.

Later on, when these troops landed on the Gallipoli Peninsula, they naturally had to rely entirely on their own resources for any kind of amenity, as no such association as the Y.M.C.A. could establish a footing immediately. Subsequently, however, as soon as it was possible to do so, your Association sent its representatives across from the adjacent islands, and was able to afford us much assistance,

Told in the Huts.

though this had to be, by force of circumstances, restricted to a very small scale—but even as such it was most welcome. On the islands of Imbros and Lemnos Y.M.C.A. depots of considerable size were established, to the great benefit of all the troops forming the Mediterranean Expeditionary Force.

Of the work of your Association in France it is quite needless for me to speak, for it is so thoroughly well-known, not only to all who have served in France, but to the Army, and indeed the public generally, in England.

Anything that can be done to help the Association to further its good work is indeed most welcome, and I most sincerely wish all success to your book for this good cause.

Yours sincerely,

W. R. Birdwood.

B. Yeaxlee, Esq., B.A.,
    Editorial Secretary, Y.M.C.A.,
        Tottenham Court Road, W.

Mine Searching

The Popular Rendezvous for Soldiers in London.

SKETCH BY SIR ROBERT BADEN-POWELL.

What it is Like at the Front Just Now.

By Sir Robert Baden-Powell.

THE country in which I now am, near Albert, consists of wide, open, rolling uplands, not a hedge to be seen, and trees only along the great high-roads or down in the hollows. The whole land is cultivated, and covered with a rime of frozen snow, across which a cutting wind is always sweeping.

Never a farm or cottage in sight; these are all clustered together in villages down in the valleys alongside the chalk streams. Barns and hay-lofts, stables and cart-sheds, form convenient billets for the men fresh from those white zig-zag lines across the hillsides—the trenches.

Here and there a smashed-up pie of a house shows that we are still within the reach of shells, but in this district every cottage has its cellars, which act as ready-made "bomb-proofs," and chalked on the wall outside one sees the legend, "Cave pour 30 hommes."

Clustered under the lee-side of the houses one sees these "hommes"—very different from the smart Tommies as we know them at home.

Workmanlike and picturesque one finds them at the Front. Muffled as they are in sheepskin woolly coats, stocking caps and mufflers, and splashed and caked with mud right up to their shoulders, one would scarcely recognise them as British soldiers were it not for the cheery though grimy faces and the remarks and songs that they keep dealing out.

* * * *

Told in the Huts.

"Rats? Plenty of them, sir! Why, they just swarm through these barns."

While he speaks of it a rat comes swanking between our feet. An officer catches him in the ribs with his stick; the dying rat turns round and looks at him with an injured expression, as though to say: "What did you do that for?" as he dies in a puddle.

"Tame? Why, only this morning my mate was lying there asleep, snoring, when I got up, and there was a rat sitting on his chest washing its face within three inches of his snore! ... No, sir, they may have eaten others, but they are not likely to eat *my* face at any rate, though they often take a bite out of my hair!"

The woodwork, the straw, and the ground itself are swarming with lice, so that between the various plagues of rats, lice and shells it is not surprising that the men get little rest.

Hot baths are arranged for in holes dug out and lined with tarpaulin, and shirts are washed in chemicals, but the results are not very permanent; just a few hours and the men are infested again.

"What do we do in the evenings? Well, there is no light after five, and fires are dangerous in the barns; the wind whistles through the walls and the sleet drives through the roof. There is only one thing to do, and that is to roll up in your blankets, and if you have any tobacco to smoke it, and to try and make the best of things with the rats outside and the lice inside. But concrete floors are not what you might call hot-beds, and are mighty hard."

Close by a pigsty with brick walls and tiled roof had been cleaned out, and within were two stretchers made of sacking and poles supported on bricks. A little brazier made out of an old tin biscuit box, and a candle stuck in a bottle, gave by contrast a comfortable atmosphere.

"You are snug enough here at any rate?"

What it is Like at the Front.

"Yes, sir. Learnt it scouting. We were Boy Scouts." But this was the exception.

* * * *

"A club, sir? If it were only a room with a dry floor and light and warmth, where one could get a cup of coffee and meet the other chaps, if would be just a godsend. We should not then be lying in our blankets in the dark, thinking of the pals that have gone, and wondering how long this fun has got to last. Why, I often feel I would rather be back in the frozen slush of the trenches. There, at any rate, you have got something doing!"

* * * *

The value of the Y.M.C.A. Huts at the front does not lie merely in their supplying the creature comforts to the soldiers; a still greater value lies behind, since they tend to keep bright in the men that splendid spirit which is just now so conspicuous at the front. It is that spirit which, I believe, is going to pull us through to victory in the end.

Napoleon long ago said that in war the moral is as three to one more powerful than the material force. Under the terrible strain on mind as well as on body, which has to be endured in the present-day warfare in the trenches, it is only reasonable to expect that the cheery spirit of our men must go down unless they can get a good change of surroundings in their rest billets.

As I have said, these rest billets are not such gaudily cheerful places as they might be. I feel, therefore, that by setting up bright, warm clubs, where the men can meet and have their fun and get their good feeding, a great step will

British Steel Helmets

Told in the Huts.

have been taken towards keeping up their spirits, and so towards tuning them up for the tremendous task which lies before them.

For this reason no effort is too great, no money ill-expended, where it is devoted to providing Recreation Huts for the Front.

[SIR ROBERT BADEN-POWELL entered his sixtieth year last February. It is forty years since he joined the Army. His active service was varied, for he served in India, Afghanistan, South Africa, Zululand, and Matabeleland. For his splendid defence of Mafeking, the close of which added a new word to the English language, he was promoted Major-General. All his life he has been fond of art, and his black-and-white work has often appeared in the illustrated papers.—ED.]

"Sweet Lavender."

By George A. Birmingham.

Was ever a name less appropriately given? I have heard of a Paradise Court in a grimy city slum, and a dilapidated whitewashed house on the edge of a Connaught bog which had somehow got itself called "Monte Carlo." But these misfits of names moved me only to mirth, mingled with a certain sadness. "Sweet Lavender" is a sheer astonishment. I hear the words, and think of the edgings of old garden borders, straggling, spiky little bushes with palely unobtrusive flowers. I think of linen cupboards, of sheets and pillow-cases redolent with very delicate perfume. I think of the women who wander through such gardens, who find a pride in their store of scented house-linen; delicately nurtured ladies, very gentle, a little tinged with melancholy, innocent, sweet. My thoughts wander through memories and guesses about their ways of life. Nothing in the whole long train of thought prepares me for, or tends in any way to suggest, this "Sweet Lavender."

It is a building. In the language of the Army—the official language—it is a Hut; but hardly more like the hut of civil life than it is like the flower from which it takes its name. The walls are of thin wood. The roof is corrugated iron. It contains two long, low halls. Glaring electric lights hang from the rafters. They must glare if they are to shine at all, for the air is thick with tobacco smoke. Inside the halls are gathered hundreds of soldiers. In one,

Told in the Huts.

French

that which we enter first, the men are sitting, packed close together at small tables. They turn over the pages of illustrated papers. They drink tea, cocoa, and hot milk. They eat buns and slices of bread and butter. They write those letters home which express so little, and, to those who understand, mean so much. Of the letters written home from camp, half at least are on paper which bear the stamp of the Y.M.C.A.—paper given to all who ask in this Hut and a score of others. Reading, eating, drinking, writing, chatting, or playing draughts, everybody smokes. Everybody, such is the climate, reeks with damp. Everybody is hot. The last thing that the air suggests to the nose of one who enters is the smell of "Sweet Lavender."

In the other, the inner hall, there are more men, still more closely packed together, smoking more persistently, and the air is even denser. Here no one is eating, no one reading. Few attempt to write. The evening entertainment is about to begin. On a narrow platform at one end of the hall is a piano. A pianist has taken possession of it. He has been selected by no one in authority, elected by no committee. He has occurred, emerged from the mass of men; by virtue of some energy within him has made good his position in front of the instrument. He flogs the keys, and above the babel of talk sounds some rag-time melody, once popular, now forgotten or despised at home. Here or there a voice takes up the tune and sings or chants it. The audience begins to catch the spirit of the entertainment. Some one calls the name of Corporal Smith. A man struggles from his seat and leaps on to the platform. He is greeted with applauding cheers. There is a short consultation between him and the pianist. A tentative chord is struck. Corporal Smith nods approval and turns to the audience. His song begins. If it is the kind of song which has a chorus, the audience shouts it, and Corporal Smith conducts the singing with wavings of his arm.

"Sweet Lavender."

Corporal Smith is a popular favourite. We know his worth as a singer, demand and applaud him. But there are other candidates for favour. Before the applause has died away, while still acknowledgments are being bowed, another man takes his place on the platform. He is a stranger, and no one knows what he will sing. But the pianist is a man of genius. Whisper to him the name of a song, give even a hint of its nature, let him guess at the kind of voice, bass, baritone, tenor, and he will vamp an accompaniment. He has his difficulties. A singer will start at the wrong time, will for a whole verse perhaps make noises in a different key; the pianist never fails. Somehow, before very long, instrument and singer get together—more or less. There is no dearth of singers, no bashful hanging back, no waiting for polite pressure. Everyone who can sing, or thinks he can, is eager to display his talent. There is no monotony. A boisterous comic song is succeeded by one about summer roses, autumn leaves, and the kisses of a maiden at a stile. The vagaries of a ventriloquist are a matter for roars of laughter. A song about the beauty of the rising moon pleases us all equally well. An original genius sings a song of his own composition, rough-hewn verses set to a familiar tune, about the difficulty of obtaining leave, and the longing that is in all our hearts for a return to "Blighty, dear old Blighty." Did ever men before fix such a name on the standard for which they fight? Now and again some one comes forward with a long narrative song, a kind of ballad chanted to a tune very difficult to catch. It is about as hard to keep track with the story as to pick up the tune. Words—better singers fail in the same way—are not easily distinguished, though the man does his best, clears his throat carefully between each verse, and spits over the edge of the platform to improve his enunciation. No one objects to that. About manners and dress the audience is very little critical. But about the

Pinnace

Told in the Huts.

merits of the songs and the singers the men express their opinions with the utmost frankness. The applause is genuine, and the singer who wins it is under no doubt about its reality. The song which makes no appeal is simply drowned by loud talk, and the unfortunate singer will crack his voice in vain in an endeavour to regain the attention he has lost.

Encores are rare, and the men are slow to take them. There is a man towards the end of the evening who wins one, unmistakably, with an inimitable burlesque of "Alice, where art thou?" The pianist fails to keep in touch with the astonishing vagaries of this performance, and the singer, unabashed, finishes without accompaniment. The audience yells with delight, and continues to yell till the singer comes forward again. This time he gives us a song about leaving home, a thing of heart-rending pathos, and we wail the chorus:

> "It's sad to be giving the last hand-shake,
> It's sad the last long kiss to take,
> It's sad to say farewell."

The entertainment draws to its close about eight o'clock. Men go to bed betimes who know that a bugle will sound the réveillé at 5.30 in the morning. The end is always the same, but always comes strangely, always as a surprise. We sing a hymn, for choice a very sentimental hymn. We say a short prayer, often as rugged and unconventional as the entertainment itself. Then "The King!" In these two words we announce the National Anthem, and the men stand stiffly to attention while they sing. At half-past eight, by order of the supreme authorities, "Sweet Lavender" Hut must close its doors. The end of the entertainment is planned to allow time for a final cup of tea or a last glass of Horlick's Malted Milk before we go out to flounder through the mud

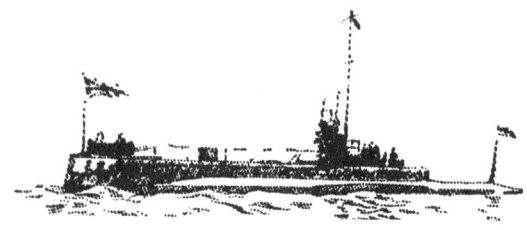

"Sweet Lavender."

to our tents. This last half-hour is a busy one for the ladies behind the counter in the outer hall. Long queues of men stand waiting to be served. Dripping cups and sticky buns are passed to them with inconceivable rapidity. The work is done at high pressure, but with the tea and the food the men receive something else, something they pay no penny for, something, the value of which to them is above all measuring with pennies—the friendly smile, the kindly word, of a woman. We can partly guess at what these ladies have given up at home to do this work—servile, sticky, dull work —for men who are neither kith nor kin to them. No one will ever know the amount of good they do; without praise, pay, or hope of honours, often without thanks. If "the actions of the just smell sweet and blossom," surely these deeds of love and kindness have a fragrance of surpassing sweetness. Perhaps, after all, the hut is well-named "Sweet Lavender." The discerning eye sees the flowers through the mist of steaming tea. We catch the perfume while we choke in the reek of tobacco smoke, damp clothes, and heated bodies. It is not every Y.M.C.A. Hut which is honoured with a name. "Sweet Lavender" stands alone here among huts distinguished only by numbers. But surely they should all be called after flowers, for in them grow the sweetest blooms of all.

Leisure Hours

Told in the Huts.

"Remember Belgium."

THEY were "somewhere" in Belgium, and the platoon to which Jim and Bill belonged was ordered to take a section of enemy trenches one cold December night, and to hold it until relieved. The snow was falling gently, had been for some days, except when it rained for a change, and they found the trenches with about three feet of water in them. Remarks were much to the point, the sergeant, eyeing the state of things critically, facetiously remarking: "Eh, lads, here's the crew, but where's the submarine?" A shell, whistling over their heads, awoke them to a sense of other discomforts, but in the same dry voice he cried, "Submerge!" and into the slime and mud and water, with gingerly steps they "submerged." Bill was lagging behind, and on Jim looking round found him firmly stuck with one leg in the sticky clay at the bottom of the trench, vainly trying to find a *point de résistance* for the other. "Jim," he exclaimed, sinking gradually, "call to mind them posters at home—'Remember Belgium'? Well, I shall never forget it. Come and pull me out!"

F. L. S.

Open to Make an Offer!

MANY thousands of Australians have recently visited London on short leave, and it has been the work of the Y.M.C.A. to sleep and feed hundreds of them. The following amusing incident occurred during the visit of one party of them. On being told in answer to his question that the charge for a bed for three nights was one shilling and sixpence, one of them exclaimed, "Lor' lumme, what'll you take for the house?"

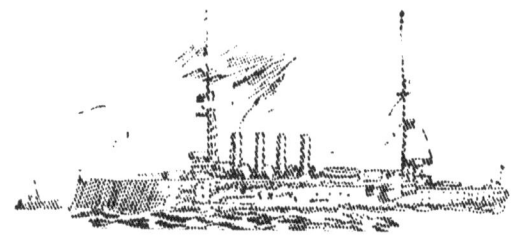

The End of the Dream

By George Goodchild.

All night long a terrific cannonade shook the very earth, and the sickly fumes of lyddite were wafted into the trenches by a damp March wind. A few star shells dropped their blue lights into the black vault of heaven, and the ubiquitous searchlight played in ghostly fashion over the devastated country. In the morning it was quiet again; hardly a sound broke the stillness save the deep rumble of artillery far to the west. The same programme, exact in every detail, was repeated day after day until men spat with exasperation at the enforced inactivity, and performed the most foolhardy tricks on the trench parapet in full view of the enemy.

"Spragge," said the corporal one evening, "did you ever think you could kill a man, deliberately and calmly?"

"Never."

"How did it come, then, the first experience?"

There was a brief silence, then the answer came slowly and softly.

"There has been no first experience—for me."

The corporal started with surprise. "How can you know that?"

"*I never shoot to hit a man.*"

The corporal shrank back, almost speechless with amazement.

"What? You tell me that!" he muttered. It was inexplicable and withal terrible. He felt a sensation

Trench Warfare

Told in the Huts.

akin to that a man feels in the presence of any abnormal being. He considered well every aspect of the question. Here were brave men filled with a common ideal, fighting for the very existence of their nation, and yet one among them, from motives which were utterly unfathomable to any ordinary being, shrunk from the duty necessity imposed upon him. He strove honestly to see things from the other's point of view. Argued from the standpoint of humanitarianism and idealism, perhaps even Christianity itself, it was unmeet to take human life coldly and deliberately, yet, he argued, there were extenuations. The enemy constituted an ever-present menace, and self-defence was always warrantable. The problem grew on his mind and tortured his few sleeping hours, yet he could not harbour the spirit of repulsion which he felt was consistent with the occasion. The quiet, big man with his massive head and delightful eloquence had impressed him in a way he had never imagined. Could such a being really be but a husk, a poor, spiritless, lifeless thing, cankered by a damning ideal? It was all too horrible. For three days he spoke not a word to Spragge.

On the morning of the fourth day the dawn broke with a magnificence unusual for the time of the year. Spragge, on his pile of bricks, watched the far horizon change from a river of red to a flood of gold, then, seeing the corporal near him, quoted:—

> "But forth one wavelet, then another, curled,
> Till the whole sunrise, not to be supprest
> Rose-reddened, and its seething breast
> Flickered in bounds, grew gold, then overflowed the world."

The corporal pretended not to hear, and commenced vigorously to clean his rifle, but a mere glance at his half-averted face was sufficient to make clear the deception.

The End of the Dream.

"What's the matter?" asked Spragge.

"Oh, nothing."

"Is it nothing that makes you shun me like the leper?"

"Have I shunned you?"

"I think it has been fairly obvious."

"Spragge!"—after a brief silence. "Why did you tell me that?"

"Tell you what?"

"You know—the other night."

"You asked me."

"Yes, yes, I know; but there were ways of evasion. Why did you make me lose my respect for you?"

Spragge looked at him curiously, then half closed his eyes in his dreamy manner.

"So you despise me for that? Despise me because I dared tell you my heart's truth. Is it so very terrible that I cannot kill in cold blood? Do you tell me that you do not hate yourself every time when you speed the bullet that takes a man's life? If I thought that you could kill and kill and be happy—knowing that you had robbed a mother of her son, a wife maybe of her husband, I would never look at you again."

"Sheer rot!" cried the other hotly. "You talk like a madman! Where is your honour—your patriotism, your——"

"Honour! Patriotism!" interrupted Spragge. "So, to save my honour I must wreck my ideals, submerge my soul in a ghastly ocean of torment and iniquity! When some poor wretch writhes in pain and agony, I must praise God because thereby my honour is upheld!"

Then he changed his tone of bitterness, and, catching hold of the corporal's sleeve, whispered, rather than spoke. "Don't judge me too harshly, Annesley, we are all God's

Zouave

Told in the Huts.

creatures, and are cast in a mould ordained for us. You don't know how it hurts. If I could act as they act" (inclining his head towards the other men), "I should save myself the acutest mental torment; but I can't, simply can't. Do you believe that?"

"Then why did you come here, where men must fight and kill and slaughter? There's a duty to be done, no matter its sternness."

"There were strange reasons. I watched day by day the stream of khaki figures streaming through the village. Each day they came and went, and each day I envied them the more. Then my mother's eyes—very soft and very grave. I could not stand their eloquent reprovals. Half the night I thought on it. Sacrifice—that is a great thing, for no evolution of ego can be perfected without it. It seemed to me that half the world was mad, and yet out of its madness grew the white flower of sacrifice, the symbol of the Cross.

"'What have I done for you, England, my England?
What is there I would not do, England, my own?'

Oh, it was all so clear and distinct—my duty—and so I came. But to kill——"

He sat down, resting his head on his hands, and the corporal, unable to control his emotion, left him.

The news crept with amazing speed through the trenches. An assault was about to begin. Men whispered to each other gleefully and yet a little nervously, and each clutched his rifle with more than usual fondness. At the back of them the roar of the massed guns was ear-splitting. The fussy sergeant-major bustled about very excitedly. "Now then, you fellows, out you come, and when you hear the whistle go, hook

Air Torpedo

The End of the Dream.

it 'hell for leather.' Make good the trenches by the trees yonder, near the brickworks."

They scrambled out of the filthy pits they had occupied for three weary weeks, and experienced the magic sensation of treading good *terra firma*, covered by the terrible fire of a wonderful artillery. Spragge stood with the rest, very pale, but very upright. The corporal walked up to him and looked at him queerly.

"I just wanted to thank you—in case——One never knows."

They gripped hands for a second, and then the whistle blew.

Off they went like hounds from the leash, whooping like wild beings, skirting shell-holes and leaping over tree-trunks which, broken and scarred, were strewn over the lacerated ground. They reached the first line of trenches, which were nothing more than an unrecognisable pit of death with dismembered corpses half hidden in the smashed soil. Hardly a soul lived to dispute the advance. At the next line of trenches it was the same—death and desolation. The havoc wrought by the massed artillery was immense, incredible. Near the village the resistance began. A dozen machine guns close by, masked in an orchard, rained a perfect hail of lead, and men dropped like ninepins. To the right a Scottish regiment were decimated by a pitiless fire which they were utterly unable to locate; yet they came on, sternly and doggedly, heads down and bayonets flashing, literally climbing over their dead in their dreadful determination. It was all very terrible, yet wonderful, and the little corporal, with a painful flesh wound, wondered where Spragge was, and forgot his own hurt and the hell in which he moved in an effort to imagine the other's feelings and sensations. Could he keep those ideals in the face of present events?

How long it lasted the corporal never knew. All

French Mountain Gun

Told in the Huts

the time he dwelt in a world far removed from that in which he ordinarily moved. Though men dropped in thousands, he experienced not one pang of remorse; it all seemed to be quite right and proper, and his mind had adapted itself to the situation with a readiness which was alarming but comforting. When eventually the whistle sounded and the fighting was over, he came to his proper state of mind in a series of connected transitions.

He moved painfully and slowly among the stretcher-bearers and ambulance wagons, and eventually found Spragge resting on a pile of sand-bags.

The latter looked at him wistfully.

"It's all over," he remarked.

"Yes. Thank God!"

Spragge wrinkled his brows and sat for a moment silent and pensive.

"It was terrible—horrible," he remarked.

"What, the fighting?"

"No. What we found in a house at the back of the church."

The corporal looked at him interrogatively. The other resumed slowly and painfully.

"She was only twenty, and she showed us what they had done to her. Oh, I can't tell you—it's too—too terrible even to relate. Her husband and child too—butchered and multilated. If—if——"

Phut! A bullet struck a sand-bag within a few inches of the corporal's chest. He started in surprise. They stepped into the shelter of a doorway and waited a few minutes. Then Spragge climbed on a heap of débris and thrust his rifle through the shell-hole. There was a loud report, and the corporal, peering round the doorway, saw in the distance a grey-clad figure drop from a tree. He turned towards Spragge.

"Eighteen!" said the latter, laconically.

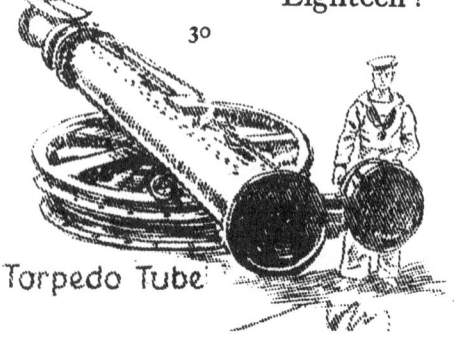

Torpedo Tube

Pro Patria.

By Rev. John Safeley, M.A.

Observation Kite

It was early on a July morning, soon after the big push north and south of the Somme had begun. The summer sun gilded the low green hills that lie round the old French seaport town, and glinted on the blue-grey waters of the Channel out beyond. The great soaring dome of the Cathedral, with its surmounting cross, looked down on us as, year in, year out, it looks down on the sloping streets and the busy harbour and the unresting sea. In the Cemetery beyond the ramparts of Hautville a little company of us stood round a long wide trench—three Army Chaplains, half a score of soldiers, three Salvationists, and one who wore the Red Triangle. About us, in seemly, flower-decked rows, daily lengthening, marked at intervals with simple wooden crosses bearing the legend, "Pro Patria," were the graves of French and British soldiers who had fallen in the war, sleeping side by side in death, as in life they had fought shoulder to shoulder. Within the trench lay three-and-twenty plain, rough coffins, each containing the battle-scarred body of a British Tommy; while two other long rows lay, earth-covered, beneath. It was holy ground—that resting-place of the heroic dead. In order of official precedence, the three Chaplains—Anglican, Wesleyan, and Roman Catholic—in quiet, solemn tones read the Burial Service, each over the men of his own communion—for even at the graveside of men who have made the supreme sacrifice our differences linger; *there*, thank God, they also

Told in the Huts.

die and are buried, never to rise again! The familiar words, poignant, comforting, hopeful, triumphant, seemed touched with a new reality. After the murmur of the Roman Priest's Latin had died away, at the word of command, the soldiers, who had been bending the while over reversed rifles, stood to attention and presented arms in seemly salute to their dead comrades, while the bugler sounded the Last Post—that call which gathers up fragments from all the bugle-calls of the day, that musical summary of a soldier's life. On one of the coffins, ere we filed silently away, the Salvationists reverently laid a bunch of summer flowers—a tribute to a comrade in their spiritual war. "*Requiescat in pace*," the Priest had murmured as he sprinkled the holy water on two of the unadorned coffins. "After life's fitful fever," echoed my heart, "they all sleep well." But their souls go marching on! Not in vain had those twenty-three been faithful unto death. Not in vain have any of the dead laid down their lives—"*pro patria et pro civitate Dei.*"

French Catapult.

A Packet of Woodbines.

By Paul Trent.

A STILL, dark night—and the lights of the hospital ship—once a famous "liner"—showed up brilliantly. A railway station with long platforms, crowded with stretcher-bearers. We, four Y.M.C.A. workers, stood at the coffee-stall, some forty yards away. Fortunately the rush had ceased, when word came that the hospital-train was drawing near.

"You had better come with me into the first carriage," said the Padre—the ideal man for the job, as I was soon to find out.

It was my first night on duty at the Quay, and I felt grateful for the suggestion. Under my arm I carried a couple of boxes of "Woodbines," and my pockets were filled with postcards. I felt a miserable coward as the train drew near and halted just outside the station. It was a heavy train and was to be divided into two portions—one for each platform.

One worker was to remain at the stall; the other, a lady, had chosen to meet the wounded with us, and she was filled with enthusiasm, enthusiasm of the right sort.

The train came along very slowly—it almost seemed as if it were trying to shake the wounded as little as possible.

"Come along," the Padre cried cheerfully—cheerfulness was his note so long as there remained work to be done.

We climbed up on to the train, an orderly opening the door for us. All my life I have tried to avoid suffering, and I felt sorely tempted to run away. On each side of the long compartment was row upon row of stretchers; on each

Reinforcements

Told in the Huts

stretcher was a wounded soldier, straight down from the Front. Eyes, many of them listless and dull, were turned towards us.

"Good morning, boys! Havre, at last—with a good ship awaiting you! And soon 'Blighty!' Who says some cigarettes?" cried the Padre.

Soon we were busily handing out cigarettes. Would anyone care to send a postcard home? Eager hands were outstretched, when hands could be moved. Dull eyes became brighter, and to us there came the great revelation—no longer were we so poignantly conscious that we were surrounded by acute suffering—that of these soldiers some had lost limbs, and that there were even those that might not live to see "Blighty." Yes, it became clear that these men were calmly courageous, and, more wonderful still—cheerful.

"What's the steamer?" asked a Tynesider.

"The ——," I answered.

"A good ship. I went home by her last time. The first time——" He broke off with a laugh. "Well, there'll be no fourth. I've lost my leg."

I gave him a light for his cigarette, and he grinned back at me.

And the youngsters were just as splendid. The smile came, although one could see that it required an effort—still it came.

"What about posting the cards? Anything to pay?"

We shook our heads. It caused a sense of shame to have to listen to thanks from such men—and for a few cigarettes and a postcard.

I chanced to notice that, although one fine chap refused a card, he appeared regretful.

"Shall I write for you? I see you have lost your hand."

He drew in a deep breath.

"No, sir—I gave it," he answered quietly.

A Packet of Woodbines.

A lump came to my throat, and I swallowed hard. This is not written to draw tears—it just happened.

Often one would have liked to linger. Ahead I could hear the Padre—he was finding many friends. How I envied him his happy touch with them. As we passed along, I gathered the impression that there was a different atmosphere with our arrival; and I soon understood the reason for it. Probably we were the first civilians they had seen for weary months, and our clothes caused them to realise that they were nearing "Blighty."

From the instant the train had stopped the R.A.M.C. had been at work—the organisation being simply magnificent—and the platforms were being rapidly covered with stretchers. All that are fit enough are smoking. Jokes are passed—and a few hours ago these men were living in an inferno.

Now and again they try to speak of their experiences, but we do not encourage them—such are better forgotten.

A glimpse of the companion-way; steadily stretchers are being carried on board, and as each man is picked up, his face brightens in spite of pain.

Now to collect the postcards. Sometimes one cannot help reading the message, with its prevailing request, "Don't worry." A total lack of regard of self—only for those at home!

Then follows the most painful visit of all—to the dressing-station for those who require immediate surgical attention. Here there is more evidence of pain, but in spite of it there is still that wonderful cheerfulness that approaches the sublime. Again the Padre has found pals, and I hear a laugh. Truly our men are wonderful, Not a grouse—it's only the slightly wounded who grumble, and then only half-heartedly.

" I gave it ! "

And they are grateful for a packet of "fags." Can we **ever** do enough for them ?

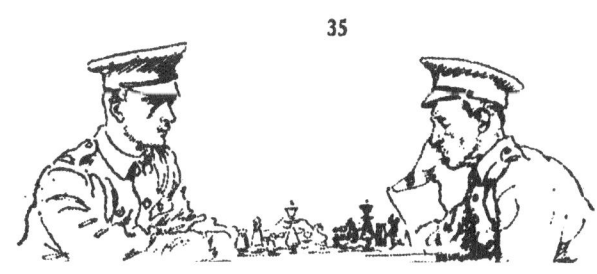

My Land.

By Betty Dundas.

O STRETCHES of moorland, with your glorious purple flowers
Set like gleaming amethysts in this grey-brown world of ours,
I close my eyes and I see you, although I am miles away,
And my heart and my mind turn to you, and are with you night and day.

I can hear the water rushing through the heather-bordered peat,
As it slipped away long years ago across my own bare feet,
My feet that pressed the brown peat, and the bog of the upland moor,
Ere I listened to the calling of this new world's golden lure.

And I stand over here in the sunshine, in the soft and sighing breeze,
And I long and long for the clouds of the North and the wind among the trees,
The wind amongst my own trees, the trees of my northern place,
The oak and the ash, and the soughing fir, and the birch with its tender grace.

The moon is up in the gloaming, and the deer steal down from the hill,
There are witches out on the moor to-night, you will see them if you keep still.
There's a coronach played on the pipes, it's playing for others and me,
Who have left their glen, and their golden land, for this other across the sea.

The Advance.

By Levorno Sabatini.

Cheero?

Official Report: " Some progress was made north of ——— after severe hand-to-hand fighting."

Over the parapet, boys, at 6.45 precisely! This long-expected order was passed along the trenches in a thrilling whisper at 6 o'clock one morning. We all looked at our wristlet watches and corrected them with each other—not one was put a minute slow—and then settled down to wait. To wait! Heavens! In forty-five minutes we were to be released from the leash that had restrained and choked us in impotence for months. We had read of the atrocities of the enemy, his war on helpless women and children at home and the destruction of defenceless ships, the "going west" of Nurse Cavell, Captain Fryatt, and of our beloved chief, and each new crime was as fuel to our pent-up rage, until we ached to exact a just retribution.

Our officers lived with us, moving up and down trenches, in and out of dug-outs, looking to our comfort before their own, sharing the privations and dangers of the first line. Their quiet courage and confidence inspired us, and we were prepared to follow them anywhere. Many times we had begged them to let us go, but the reply was always— "No, boys, not yet! Your time will come." Aye, but what a long time coming! Yet those weary months seemed but as fleeting moments in comparison with the awful nerve-racking suspense of those forty-five minutes.

Told in the Huts.

Winter at the Front

The Padre moved among us, imparting words of cheer and advice. Some there were who wrote a few lines home, others hurriedly scrawled their long-neglected last will and testament (most reading, " I leave all to my dear wife ") on scraps of paper to be posted in certain eventualities, for we were about to face the great unknown, and were under no illusion as to what it might mean. The point of view veers to different things at a time like this. The *soul* of the man comes out, and his thoughts are simple—just of home and what *might* be. The good man gave his assurance that those scraps of paper should be sacredly dealt with were they not reclaimed by the owners.

Thus the minutes ticked by—one by one—to the accompaniment of the thunder of guns, beginning the task which we were to finish.

6.43. We were silent and tense with excitement, and a curious feeling of detachment from ourselves came over us. No thought now of anything but the job in hand possessed us, while the batteries lengthened their range, keeping up a curtain fire of death-dealing missiles beyond our immediate objective.

"*Over you go, boys !*" put an end to our suspense, and with glistening bayonets up the trench we clambered, over the sand-bag parapet, and across that death-pitted " No Man's Land " towards the section of the enemy's first line we were to take. This we reached and occupied easily; so effective had been our artillery, that nothing animate remained in them, with the exception of one dug-out where a few dazed Huns remained huddled together murmuring, " Kamarade, Kamarade," with hands up, all spirit of fighting gone. Up came the supports, and away to the second and third system of defence works, gradually meeting fiercer resistance by grenade and machine gun. Our boys were mad now with the lust of battle—yelling, cursing, praying—bombing and bayoneting their way up this trench, down that,

The Advance.

clearing dug-outs which were turned from places of safety into traps of death.

Many incidents occurred which cannot be recorded; but one stands out prominently. Our boys had come upon a crater caused by a mine, and occupied by the enemy. It simply *had* to change hands, so into it with bayonet we went. Our captain led us furiously, snatching a rifle with fixed bayonet from one of our wounded. Gradually we gained the upper hand, and the last fight was with a burly Hun and our captain. Exhausted, and with even at that moment a sense of fair-play, we watched the hand-to-hand struggle. At last the enemy went down with a clever half-nelson, and our captain, one foot on him, raised his bayonet to administer the *coup de grace*, when, to our surprise, he flung it aside, murmuring, " I can't do it. Hang it all, he was a sport ! " and kneeling down by the side of his antagonist, he gave him a drink from his own water-bottle. Thus do Britons conquer but do not crush.

We had been fighting all day, and in expectation of the counter-attack which inevitably comes, we worked all night under a terrific bombardment, repairing the damaged trenches we had gained. In the grey mists of the early morning it came. Wave after wave surged against our sadly thinned ranks, but bravely we held out with rifle and machine-gun fire, expecting the reinforcements promised at any moment. Then clouds of poisonous gas were released by the enemy, rising and falling like a grey curtain, but passing over our heads harmlessly in the gentle breeze. Gradually, however, we were pressed back yard by yard before that diabolical stuff and the furious onslaughts of the reinforced enemy, retiring to a deep cutting which led to excavations in the chalk cliff where caves and caverns had been formed and where we knew our reinforcements should be. And there we found them !—*gassed to a man!* The hellish fumes had been sucked down into that cutting and

The Optimist

Told in the Huts.

had been blown into the caves and holes in thick clouds and suffocated them all. There they were—a pathetic sight, in all attitudes. Some leaning on their rifles with head bent on breast, others laying face-down on the cold dank ground, nipped off in the strength of manhood without a chance to defend themselves. But they could be avenged, and with a mad cry to God our brave boys turned as one man and charged full pelt at the advancing enemy. In that moment they were supermen, and nothing could withstand them. The enemy, taken by surprise at the sudden and unexpected onslaught, broke and fled, leaving their dead and wounded to mark their trail. Yet on and on they went, one by one falling wounded and dying, until not one of that brave band of British warriors was left, and not one returned except on a stretcher. But they had exacted a terrible retribution, and the reserves following up, consolidated the ground won by such heroism and self-sacrifice.

The Official Report read:

> "Some progress was made north of —— after severe hand-to-hand fighting."

But it was the talk and admiration of the British Army in trench, dug-out, and hut for many a day afterwards.

Posting Home

"It was Me, Sargint!"

By One of the Third Line.

The Army is one of the most enlightening places in the world in which to look for examples of bearing one another's burdens. That is not to say there is a waiting list of those who jostle for their places in fatigue squads, but that the powers have decreed that one man shall be responsible for the misdeeds of a certain number of others.

Is the N.C.O. in charge of No. 1 Pioneer squad a saint from heaven? Has he a University degree? Was he first of his year? Let that be. "Sir, I have the honour to report that in B Company's lines, between Hut number umpty-two and Hut number umpty-three, at 10.55 a.m., the following articles, viz., one empty salmon tin, two square pieces of paper, and one round piece, were found by me, as orderly officer of the day." That's it all. A severe Rep. for the N.C.O. of No. 1 Pioneers, and not a whisper of scandal to besmirch the fair name of Private Skipit, who shirked his bit of work.

Or take this, souvenired from an attack of "Lectures to N.C.O.'s": "If a man comes unshaven on parade *you're* to blame. It's *your* job. You N.C.O.'s are far too slack, and it's high time . . . and if you don't . . ." Muggins' bed is not made down at 6.45 a.m. The straw still sticks aggressively out from his canvas pillow; his blankets sprawl in a shapeless heap on the floor, where he left them. But then Muggins is a cook, goes to business at 3 a.m., and the Army in these parts drills on its breakfast. He must stick

Battleship

Told in the Huts.

to his post until the last square inch of bacon disappears from his view for ever. He returns at 9 a.m., happy after work well done, whistles as he folds his blankets according to pattern No. 8A, the while his Hut Sergeant, flanked by two escorts with bayonets fixed, trembles before the blast of the O.C.'s wrath, then gasps with relief to learn that he is let down lightly with a paltry fine of two days' pay.

Thus, by mutual burden-bearing, are the Army's statutes kept.

" What pussles me," said Macdonald from Skye, " iss the principle off it all. If Sarchints iss responsible for prifates, then Comp'ny Officers iss anserable for Sarchints. And who iss it that gifs the Company Officers orders, whateffer ? The Achutent, Yess—and the C.O. tells the Achutent— effery crime that a man's crimet for, on a principle o' that way off workin' goes right away pack to the shoulders of the C.O.—and it's the big choke it'll pe to see the C.O. and the Achutent cleekin' at the touple when the defaulter's pugle plows ! "

That is one side of the vicarious element in soldiering, and here is the other. The foregoing refers to the unwilling variety ; but the following incident reveals a higher, better kind—*i.e.*, when it is *not* looked at from the officer's point of view.

We were on guard. It was two o'clock on a pitch-black morning streaked murky-white with sleet. The guardroom was furnished with a stove that gave the lie direct to the proverb that where there's smoke there's fire. Our stove was all smoke and no fire. We coughed and shivered, and tried to snatch a few minutes of " tired nature's sweet restorer," when there came a smart tapping on the window that made us start. The sergeant opened the door and blinked in the flare of a flash-lamp. Then, from somewhere at the heart of that brilliance that cut through the outer darkness like a stab, the voice of the captain of the day

"It was Me, Sargint!"

issued, tuned to one of those five-flat keys that betoken woe to somebody (and usually vicarious woe at that), "Where's No. 3 Post?"

"No. 3's the coal wagons, sir!" said the Sergeant, looking round, and discerning in a corner by the stove, Private James Flynn, who at that moment should have been on No. 3 post.

"Coal wagons? Yes. Well, there's nobody there!"

The Orderly Officer was plainly riled.

"Beg pardon, sir! I posted that relief myself at 1.30. The wagons are well along the sidings now, sir—perhaps——"

"You say you posted it yourself?—'m. Send one of your men to show the way—it's so confoundedly dark"—that, be it understood, is merely an approximation to the real remark—"I may have made a mistake."

The Sergeant looked. "Smith," said he, "you are detailed to point out No. 3 Post to Ord'ly Officer."

Out went Smith, and all was quiet as the door was gently pushed to from the inside. The Sergeant looked round. "A volunteer, for the love of heaven. Who's the sprinter among you? Here, grab that rifle and bayonet, and come on—I'll tell you on the way."

Two figures went stumbling, pell-mell, through the murk, and made a flanking movement past the officer and his guide—a very well executed movement if you remember that the itinerary included such interesting obstacles as two rows of barbed wire fence, one spiked gate, and one artillery parade ground, two feet deep in mud.

The officer was skilfully led by his guide—the more skilfully because the guide had duly noted the sergeant's meaning look as they had set out. As they came near to the wagons they heard the steady tramp of sentry's feet. Then a clear, full-toned voice rang out, "Halt, who comes there?"

* * * * * *

Stand

Told in the Huts.

The guard-room door swung open once more, and as the sergeant re-entered his eye travelled round the circle of eager faces.

"Flynn, you blighter, y'see the hullabaloo you've raised?"

"Sure," said Flynn, "it was me, Sargint, and it's chilled to the bone I was guardin' empty wagons, and knowin' yez were sleepin', I slipped back—like an'——"

"That'll do, Flynn. But, praise the pigs, you just missed it! It'd take months of field punishment No. 2 to wipe *that* out—Gee, but it was narrow!"

And so, as was said, by mutual burden-bearing, the great British Army pursues its stately course.

Mortar

A Bit of Bunting.

By a Wounded Anzac.

Observation Kite

They have settled the ward for the evening,
   And straightened every bed;
We have drunk our bowls of cocoa,
   And they've covered the lights with red.
We are lying now till the morning—
   'Tis a terrible time to wait,
When the day seems twenty-four hours
   And the night seems forty-eight.
For the man to the right is restless,
   I can hear him mutter and moan,
And the boy in the bed beside me
   Is breaking his heart for home.
I doze a little at moments,
   Till I'm back with the heat and flies
In the sniper's line of fire,
   With the sunlight in my eyes.
It's curious, lying thinking,
   When the clock strikes once and again,
How fate has formed us together
   In a regiment of pain;
How from far-off town and village,
   From the peace of the country sward,
We have answered the call of England—
   To meet again in a ward!

Told in the Huts.

Come to the Cook House, Boys

You have heard of the old pied piper
   Who came to the village street,
And played a tune to the children,
   A melody strange and sweet;
And with eyes aglow with laughter,
   And curls that shone in the sun,
They tramped to the sound of the music,
   And followed him every one.
We all grow bitter at seasons—
   God knows we are battered and worn—
And we feel in our darkest moments
   That nothing more can be borne;
But say what you will about it,
   There is something in each man's breast
That would urge him to rise and follow,
   Though he hungered for peace and rest.
It is stronger than home and comfort,
   It is stronger than love and life,
Than the speechless grief of a mother
   Or the clinging arms of a wife;
For whenever the old flag shall summon,
   In the midst of his direst pain,
He would hear it out of the shadows,
   And it would never call in vain.

Do we wonder why we have done it
   When the pain is hardest to bear,
And the helpless years to come
   Press like a load of care?
Do we wonder why we have done it,
   When just at the break of day
We fancy we hear the sobbing
   Of the loved ones far away?
Over the mantel yonder,
   Between the glass and the wall,

A Bit of Bunting.

They have wedged a piece of bunting—
  You can scarcely see it at all;
But my eyes go searching for it
  Before they cover the light,
For it's brought a message with it,
  And I read it every night;
For whether he's tired and weary,
  Or whether he's hurt and sad,
Or whether he's old and helpless,
  Or whether he is but a lad,—
As long as England is England,
  And as long as a man has his will,
He would rise from a bed of sickness
  To hobble after it still.

They say that the grandest picture
  In England, when war is done,
And we've dragged our own from the Germans,
  And fought and bled and won,
Will not be the row of medals
  That blaze on a general's breast,
Or the little letters of glory
  That follow a hero's name;
But the sight that will rouse the nation
  And stir our pulses yet,
The sight that the women of England
  Will count as a lasting debt,
Is the empty sleeve of a soldier
  Who has braved the surgeon's knife,
And the man who goes on crutches
  For the rest of his mortal life.

"Dead Beat"

Behind the Lines.

By the Hon. Mrs. Stuart Wortley.

It was the dinner-hour in our Hut, somewhere in France. The morning had been a busy one; fresh stores had come in with hardly time to check them, and fill up the stock before "opening." The "rushes" were overwhelming at times; the Brigade was on the move, and by nightfall would be stealing silently in the dark westwards. It meant "good-bye" to all the familiar faces of the past month, and by to-morrow we should look across the counter at fresh ones, hear fresh accents, but always the same honest, grateful smiles and quick responsiveness would be sure to meet us. Days like this string us up to breaking-point.

A knock came at my door. "Come in," I said, and Mary Smith entered. I saw at a glance it was the last straw with her. She had just lost a brother, so no wonder.

"My time is up on Monday," she said, "and I must go, Mr. B——. It is no good my staying, I feel so useless."

"Are you tired?" I said.

"Not physically, but mentally. I feel like a street that has been incessantly trampled on and worn out, so many feet have shuffled by, so many heavy boots with weary tread. I hear them in my sleep." She paused, and her lip quivered. "I am tired with the constant procession of faces, faces with sad eyes and smiling lips; they haunt me; the sing-songs and the cheery laughter break my heart. I can't bear it any longer." She made a gesture of despair, and went on a little excitedly: "What is so dreadful is the background of

Behind the Lines.

tragedy and the futility of what one does. I can't see a man now laying in a stock of cigarettes or buying boot polish or "Bluebell" without thinking that in a few days he will be lying out somewhere in the night-time and the cold with the life-blood oozing out and making a black patch beside him. It is then one would like to help them. Why can't one be a stretcher-bearer and save them from the loneliness and pain and death?

"And then the sights you see here. The poor fellow who used to wander in looking for his brother who had been killed; every day he came and sat watching the door. Of course he had lost his wits, but it was some weeks before he was sent home, and he spent most of his time in here, because it was the last place he had seen his brother.

"Then there were those three pals we used to call Athos, Porthos, and d'Artagnon. Never apart. Do you remember the night they pledged each other in tea that one would not come back without the others? Porthos and d'Artagnon, we heard afterwards, fell at Ypres together, and Athos was wounded and died in hospital. I tell you, it is the very threshold of death, and you expect me to go on handing cups of tea and packets of chocolate across the counter as though it was a Church bazaar for an additional curate's fund!"

I said nothing, letting her pour out all her pent-up feelings.

"I have seen over and over again men sob as they try to write the last letter home that they will ever write—and they know it, too. It is supposed that a soldier is always jolly and cheerful because he thinks the other fellow may get killed, but not he. I tell you these men have made the great renunciation; their eyes are full of it, it is at the back of their minds while they smoke and sing and chaff. And what can you do for them? Tragedy one side of the bar, and utter futility the other. Think of all the strength, the

Welcome

youth, the splendid manhood that comes in and out of these doors, and one can't raise a finger to save them from agony of mind or body.

"In a hospital, at any rate, one can fight for their lives, relieve the pain, speak to them; but here, behind the lines, there is a conspiracy of silence, a sort of pretence that no one is thinking of what happens out yonder, and that soldiering is just routine varied by a sing-song.

"It is that dumb agony that my soul cries out against. I feel like putting my back to the door and shouting, 'You shan't go—you shan't go—it is all a nightmare, and you are free to go home by to-morrow's boat.' Home, yes, real home! not that pretence, that mockery, 'A home away from home.' It is all diabolical."

Poor Mary! I ought to have sent her straight to bed with a sleeping draught instead of trying clumsily to explain things. She had been one of our best workers for three months, and I didn't want to lose her.

"But, Mary," I said, "we are trying to help these men in the best way we can. I know it is very little we can do, but if you have ever stood by a death-bed you will realise how little human help avails when the supreme moment comes; and if you do look upon the scene of your work as the ante-chamber of death, and can give just the services that are required by those who have to face the great ordeal, be content to do so, quietly, methodically, unemotionally, just as you would do in a sick room. I think you are helping to create an atmosphere that will soothe and strengthen and comfort the men who pass through.

"I believe, as you say, a great many men have made the great renunciation, and perhaps the bitterness is past; they realise, too, that war does not multiply the sum total of deaths. It has only brought death nearer and made it the greatest reality of life, instead of a shadowy possibility.

"But," I added, "if your nerves are all to pieces—and

Behind the Lines.

I know you have had a shock which would account for their being so—why not go home, and try Y.M.C.A. work in one of the big military training camps? There, I think, you would find the 'Home away from home' phrase anything but a mockery, for I am convinced that the freshly-joined recruit finds in the Hut a little niche for himself and a welcome, and the easy-going freedom of a home; or go to a railway station Hut in London, and see for yourself how you help in driving out the demon of depression by giving the weary and downcast traveller a good bed and a solid meal. If a man is going back to the Front from furlough, material comfort and a welcome are the best cures for home-sickness. Coming home from the Front, too, has its dangers when you think of the sharks in the streets of the great unknown wilderness of the Metropolis. Or why not go to a munition factory? You can be quite sure of not being futile when you are helping to feed the weary munition worker—man or woman—who probably had to get up at four a.m. to be at work at seven, and but for a Y.M.C.A. dining-room would be eating his or her sandwich out of a greasy paper, sitting on a kerbstone in the street, not because he hadn't money in his pocket, but because of the absence of restaurants. Talking of tragedy, I know girls who are wearing a halo of gold round their heads now, and are rapidly qualifying for representation in painted glass windows."

"How do you mean?" said Mary.

"Why, girls of eighteen and nineteen are being dyed bright yellow, hands and face and hair and skin, by the powder they work in, and are quietly taking their turn, in fortnightly shifts, in the 'danger factory,' where explosions take place quite frequently. You can't get away from tragedy, in its way. I don't think there is a sight more tragic than these thousands of young women and girls dedicating their health, their energies, their youth to the work of destruction—they whose joy and glory should be life-giving.

Told in the Huts.

"But if these things have to be, it is no use getting morbid about them. The only thing is to mitigate the discomfort, the weariness, and the loneliness of the great effort men and women are making. The simplicity of an action is not always the measure of its greatness. The Samaritan's act was not a sensational one, yet the record of it has been an example for two thousand years. I am not sure the 'service' rendered by the Y.M.C.A. to men of all classes and creeds and races within the Empire may not prove as strong a cement in building up a new community as the idea of Imperialism. It has revealed men to each other in a new light."

Mary was gazing out of the window at the empty packing-cases.

"It is lunch time," she said, "and after lunch I want to scrub the counter."

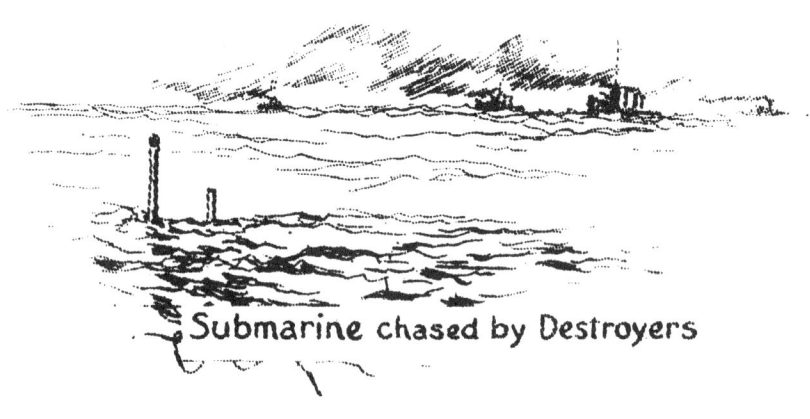
Submarine chased by Destroyers

An Exchange of Favours.

By Eric De Banzie.

If anyone asks Pte. Bill Holmes the time, *nolens volens*, he's his friend for life. . . . You're curious? I'm delighted to be able to tell you the reason.

In the days before the Allies commenced Big Pushing it was the keen desire of practically every regiment in the British Army to be placed opposite the mild and friendly Saxons. Thus the Tommies were assured of a comparative rest, and a tin of bully-beef could readily be exchanged for a passable cigar. If the enemy sent out a working party to repair their entanglements, we sent out another to rebuild the parapets battered and smashed by " whizz-bangs," and in possession of the welcome knowledge that not a shot would be fired.

This lack of the " strafing " propensity, it will be understood, was anathema to our Brass Hats, so when the men of the 5th Blankshires were informed that the General of their Brigade was coming to inspect their trenches, they immediately decided that a small " strafe " was necessary.

Unfortunately, however, it happened that a fat officer of the German Army, weary of a dark dug-out, chose that very morning to sun himself, seated in a comfortable arm-chair, on the top of the trench parapet! This implied a striking trust in the fair-play of the 5th Blankshires, but unhappily the compliment came at an inopportune moment, and eventually Pte. Bill Holmes, the look-out man, popped his

Told in the Huts.

head over the top and excitedly signalled to the fat German officer to get down and go away.

The German officer regarded his gesticulations kindly, but did not move; so Bill procured a board, frequently used to convey messages to our friend the enemy, and indulged in linguistic exercises.

"Alley toot sweet," he wrote—which, in case you don't know, is French for "Go away at once"—adding, as an afterthought, the English equivalent, "Hop it quick!"

Herr Lieutenant shook his head uncomprehendingly, but smiled to atone for his ignorance.

Things were getting desperate. The Brigadier would be round at any moment, and Bill knew that if he saw a German lolling in calm security in the open he certainly would not be polite to the look-out man. . . . Accordingly, Pte. Holmes, after a spasm of concentrated thought, raised his rifle to his shoulder, taking careful aim at the fat German officer's big toe. He fired. The range was short; there was a wild howl as the chair toppled backwards, and the German disappeared with a somersault into his trench! . . .

Half an hour afterwards, when the satisfied General had been gone barely five minutes, Bill Holmes observed a message-board being pushed above the German trenches. With the help of his friends he deciphered the writing on it:

"Who shot our officer?"

"Charlie Chaplin," suggested Snooker Brown.

They all laughed—except Holmes.

"I don't see anyfink to laugh at," said he, uneasily. "They p'r'aps mean to work off this 'ere vendetter stunt on me."

"Well, let 'em," said Snooker, valiantly. "I'll back you up."

So Bill wrote for the Huns' perusal: "Me—Bill Holmes."

In the trench next morning a small package was found,

An Exchange of Favours.

to which was tied a label bearing the words: "To Mr. Bill Holmes." It was pointed out to the addressee, who picked it up gingerly.

"From Fritz," explained Snooker Brown expectantly, edging away. . . . "Don't open it, you fathead—it'll go off!"

Holmes looked at it as a dog looks at a cat.

"Well, wot d'you fink I should do wif it?" he asked; but there was no reply. Bill was alone. His comrades were deep in the bowels of the earth listening for the bang.

At last he decided. With trembling fingers he opened the package—to find therein a magnificent gold watch, heavy but elegant, and a short letter. He read the letter; then scratched his head in puzzled astonishment.

"Blimey," he said at last; "them blokes is almost human!"

For this is what he read:—

"My good friend,—I send you the enclosed gift as a small token of my sincere thanks. You have to-day accomplished—is my spelling correct?—what I have been praying for for weeks. The wound is not serious, but now I shall be sent home for a time to see again my so-loved wife and children. So you see your so-much-to-be-admired shooting was kind to me. Good-bye."

And that is why if you ask Pte. Bill Holmes, of the 5th Blankshires, to tell you the time, and give him the opportunity to display a magnificent gold watch—heavy but elegant—you're his friend for life.

A Motor Patrol boat

The V.C. Padre

(Rev. Noel Mellish).

By A. Gordon Hamlin.

The Morning.

Early one morning we saw him. 'Twas in our Hut, and he was officiating at a specially arranged service of Holy Communion. There were many men present, kneeling there, reverently, silent before the Cross. When night came they knew that they would be making a charge. That early service was an intense moment for Chaplain, men, and for us.

The Evening.

We saw them again in the evening. The whole battalion marched past on their way to the trenches; forward to the task given them by their general. The boys were splendidly confident, swinging along the road to a tune they were whistling. Marching with them, carrying his pack as they were theirs, went the Padre, to share " the job " with the men.

The Next Day.

Just before dawn the guns began to speak. It was a terrific bombardment. Suddenly it ceased, and then we knew that the Fusiliers were " in it." How could we help earnestly praying for them ?

Down came a messenger—the Chaplain had sent him for a box of chocolate—Mr. Mellish would pay later (as if

The V.C. Padre.

we cared about that!). He had been simply wonderful helping with the injured, and wanted the chocolate for some wounded who were out in a cruelly exposed place and could not be brought in until nightfall. Yes, the boys had done well, but he must hurry back with the chocolate!

Our Hut remained open all the next night, for the men who had so gallantly carried out " the job " had been relieved and were straggling back in two's and three's. What tales they related, grouped around our big stove, warmed as well by a cup of tea and a welcome smoke!

" That Chaplain of ours—man, you should have seen him!" said one of the group around the stove. And then he added a sentence that was prophetic: " He'll get the V.C., you mark my words."

And he did!

*Yours very sincerely,
Noel Mellish CF
4th Royal Fusiliers*

By the way love for a box of chocolate which we took up for our wounded.

[FAC-SIMILE OF PART OF LETTER WRITTEN BY THE REV. NOEL MELLISH REFERRING TO THE CHOCOLATES THE MESSENGER WAS SENT FOR.]

The Lighter Side.

By Geo. R. Jenkins.

At our No. 3 Tent in Richmond we had the services of an old Orderly placed at our disposal, and after some experience we are not at all sure that we feel particularly grateful to the O.C., but rather have a lurking suspicion that the Company Officer was delighted with the opportunity to shift the responsibility of "Old Tom" on to our shoulders. His attempts at cookery were execrable, and his work a supreme illustration of the "muddle through" policy. This, therefore, added to our enjoyment of the joke when one morning the Leader and his chum, two fiery "theologicals," invited Tom to morning devotions. Old Tom shook his head, and with the "you can't catch an old bird expression" replied, "Excuse me, sir, but I belongs to the Church."

* * * * *

On another occasion, orders were issued that all men were to attend weekly bathing parade in the lake close by; Tom asked the Leader if he could have a hot bath now and again, in our bath, and so be excused the official performance. The Leader wrote the Company Officer, and received the reply:— "I do not object, providing you see the Orderly gets his bath, because he has a reputation for preferring godliness to cleanliness." After the previous incident of the prayers and our experience of Old Tom, this was a perfect scream.

* * * * *

I suppose the somewhat apocryphal story of the lady who served a packet of "Selso" seidlitz powders to the poor Tommy who asked for "Soldiers' Friend" (a button polish) is well-known in Y.M. circles.

An Orderly

Ten Days.

By Pte. J. C., K.R.R.

Off Duty

My part in the war has certainly been more exciting than spectacular. When I think of the months of toil and the strenuous work of training, it makes me grind my teeth to think of the wicked waste of time and the agonies which I endured all for a few days of trench warfare—for I was knocked out in exactly ten days from my first introduction to the trenches, and all the Drill Sergeant's curses and patience were exhausted to no apparent purpose. But I suppose my poor little bit is somewhere sandwiched in the huge patchwork quilt of war which the millions of personal experiences go to make up, and although it may be invisible to ordinary vision, yet there is some small consolation in the knowledge that it is there nevertheless.

We embarked at Southampton and made the voyage to Havre in painfully short time, convoyed by a few vicious little torpedo-boats which performed the most extraordinary tactics—rushing about like mad at one moment, and then turning about and meandering at apparent leisure. They always seemed to me to be chuckling with wicked glee. I can't tell why it struck me that way, but it did.

Overhead a couple of seaplanes spun in the sunlight like dragon-flies, turning in circles, and watching for lurking U boats. All the men were full of high spirits and joking about the future, but underneath the superficial gaiety of some of them it was easy to observe a sense of deep foreboding. A few hours ago many of them had said good-bye to wives and children on the station platform. It was impossible

Told in the Huts.

that they should feel the gayness they pretended to enjoy. There was a queer look in the eyes and an occasional nervous movement of the lips, which expressed their deeper emotions. How I thanked God I had no wife or child!

For fourteen days we were billeted in a little French village just behind the firing-line, where we practised bomb-throwing, and incidentally learned that *pain* was bread and that beer had no material French equivalent. Then the inevitable rumour went round—we were going up into the trenches! Of course, no one believed it—it never pays to believe rumours in the Army, they are as frequent and numberless as the vermin in a front-line dug-out. But it proved to be true, and up we went to relieve a badly mauled Scotch regiment. The memorable experience of the ensuing ten days is roughly as follows :—

Tuesday.

Arrived in a perfect labyrinth of trenches. Pouring with rain and ground nothing less than a quagmire. Felt a terrible inward sinking, as though all my courage had oozed out. Took over the section of trench from a party of "Jocks," so covered from head to foot with mud it was almost impossible to recognise their uniforms. A brawny Scot chuckled at the sight of our irrepressible nervousness and assured us we should soon get used to it. Nothing but mud and water. Parapets all down. Was told off to repair them. Put kit in dug-out, a dark musty hole, also wet and smelling abominably. Commenced work with spade, piling up sand-bags, heavy as lead. Two hours later—first shell arrived. Heard it two minutes before it alighted, and wondered where it would fall. Dived in dug-out and heard the beastly thing explode about fifty yards away. Recommenced work and eventually succeeded in making the trench ship-shape. Everything very quiet. Went to bed, but could not sleep. Place infested with vermin.

Destroyer

Ten Days.

Wednesday.

Beautiful morning. Surprised to hear birds singing in a wood to the right. Eight o'clock, shells commence to arrive. Began to discern the different shrieks of the various kinds. There was one which came through the air with the noise of a traction-engine. When it alighted, the earth shook in a most terrifying way. Fortunately none came near enough to show its real capabilities. Four o'clock, shrapnel shell exploded in middle of trench. Two men killed, seven injured. Felt sick at first, but later experienced a new sensation—anger and blood-thirst. Amazed to find my first " funk " had almost entirely evaporated.

Thursday.

Beginning to reconcile the situation. No more retreats to dug-out except when the " traction-engines " announce their early arrival. Comparative quiet all the afternoon. Thought over the whole thing and concluded that it was not quite so bad as I first imagined. Began to consider risk of injury in true proportion. Reckoned my chance of getting killed at 100 to 1 against, per month—wounded 10 to 1. Bucked up considerably.

Friday.

Had a glimpse of " No Man's Land " for first time through a trench periscope. An amazing sight. Earth pounded to atoms—all heaps and holes. Trees shorn of all branches and splintered cruelly. Long grass growing out of the muck-heaps, and here and there bodies of men, mercifully half-hidden in the grass. I wondered why they had not brought them in, but was told that no armistice was permitted by either side, and out there it was death sure and certain.

Told in the Huts.

Saturday.

Treated to first sight of the enemy. Man in enemy trench waved white flag and then climbed over parapet. Told us they were Saxons and had just taken over trench from Prussian Guard. Apparently not in love with Prussians. Told us they would not fire on us if we'd promise likewise. Spoke English perfectly. All day spent in bringing in dead. Buried them behind trench. Awful business! Saxons very decent. Swopped cigarettes and newspapers. Lieutenant translated some articles from *Lokal-Anzeiger*. Awful lot of lies judging from our own papers.

Sunday.

Not a shot all day. Saxons singing hymns.

Monday.

Great stir everywhere. Something in the wind. British artillery at it all day. Mid-day big Saxon threw over note wrapped round a stone. Learned from contents that Prussian Guard were relieving Saxons immediately. Told us to lie low. Later, Prussians arrive and started firing. Later in evening a party of enemy bombers attacked us. One man came right up to trench and threw six. Tremendous scuffle, but brought him down, luckily.

Tuesday.

Artillery worse than ever. Enemy very active. All day on the *qui vive*. Received reinforcements and wondered why.

Wednesday.

Heard reason for activity. Told we were "going over" early in morning. Everybody very excited. Received three days' rations late in the evening. Felt a miserable coward but glad to get at them, nevertheless. Best chum "went west" through a bomb—madder than ever.

Bursting Shell

Ten Days.

Thursday.

The fatal day here! Received instructions just before dawn. Told to take opposite trench and hold until No. 2 party arrived to consolidate, then to go forward to second line and hold until further instructed. Artillery going like mad, never heard anything like it. Got order and went over top. Could see shells pounding the enemy trench to atoms. Felt better by the sight. Suddenly noise lifted and a queer silence prevailed. My heart seemed to stand still. Could not see trench ahead, owing to smoke and dust. Then the order came and we went forward at the double with the bayonet. Everyone yelled like mad, and the sound was extraordinarily comforting. Soon lost all sense of surroundings, and doubled like one in a dream. I shall never forget the next quarter of an hour. It was a horrible nightmare that will always cling. Men were going down like ninepins, maxims crackling, and amid all the strange, rare sounds of battle nothing seemed so penetrating as the human voice. A man laughed idiotically, and it seemed to ring right above the din of guns, and yet as far away as the sounds that come when one is under the anæsthetic, just on the brim of unconsciousness.

We took that trench and held it—how, I don't know. But there I found myself amid the rubbish and dead men, muttering a word again and again in a ridiculous fashion.

Then I felt terribly sick and faint, and a cold sweat came out all over me. This I utterly failed to understand till a Corporal came up and put his arm round my shoulder. I saw him look at something on my chest, and, astonished, I turned my eyes down—a bullet had gone clean through me, and two of my fingers were missing—and I never knew a thing about it until then!

* * *

Home again in glorious "Blighty," and waiting for my discharge. It's a grand change, and I'm glad I've done my bit—small though it be.

The Ghastly Experience of a 2nd Lieutenant.

By Capt. H. Harrop.

Firing Rifle Grenades

I AM very sorry that I did not tell you how, when, and where I got my little dose, but you will remember that my first inquiries when I got here were chiefly for cake and clothes, and I got so sick of telling people all about it, that I thought you surely must have been one of the many to whom I detailed "ye hystorie of my woes." I am afraid that I cannot describe it with the pathos of the "Oh, was-not-it-beastly-ness?" that I could have a week or two ago, as I am feeling much better now; but it will doubtless be a saner account.

You will know that there has been three great attacks on the push front so far—July 1st, 14th, and 22nd. On the 1st, as far as I can remember, the battery was in our new position, south of Arras, at Wailly, ready for the show, but at the last moment the attack on the Arras-Gommecourt was cancelled and we trekked south. On the 14th we were in reserve and saw most of the fighting for Contalmaison and in Montauban and Trones Wood; we were moved to Montauban about the 17th, and had our Brigadier-Major killed by shrapnel as soon as we got up on the ridge. Two valleys end at Fricourt, one going S.E. to Comoy, one east to Longueval and Delville Wood, which are at the top of the valley, and there is another valley running from Longueval N.W. to Bayentin-le-Grand. Our head-quarters, just west

The Ghastly Experience of a 2nd Lieutenant.

of Montauban, on the top of the ridge, were under continual shell-fire. The valley (H.F.) was full to the eyes with our guns and Bosche shells, and along the northern ridge of the same valley was the old Bosche second line; then, more north still, came the Longueval to Bayentin Valley, and across that—two miles away—was Highwood, Pozieres. What we were after was Highwood and the sunken road between it and Delville Wood. I went up into the trenches we were holding on the 20th (the old Bosche second line on the N.E. ridge of Gun Valley) and watched the Gordons attack Highwood from our side of the valley in the early morning mist. They were mown down in dozens, but at the end of the day we held a line from between Pozieres and Bayentin, along the west edge of Highwood and down to Longueval. You will see that we were on the crest of the ridge, which on our brigade front was the sunken road. Fritz had a battery of maxims at M.G. on the corner of the Wood and absolutely enfiladed the sunken road just behind, and east of which were his trenches. The distance from our trenches to the sunken road was about 350 yards, all corn and long grass and shell-holes. The brigade was to advance and take the sunken road at 1.30 A.M. on the night of the 22nd-23rd, and my job was to smash the guns at M.G., the east corner of the Wood. After a lot of casualties among the carrying parties, I managed to get four guns and five hundred shells up to (G), a point about two hundred yards from Fritz's guns, and out in the open, well away from the Wood, which was being shelled to blazes continually. We were in the open field with no possible cover of any sort, with shrapnel coming over ten a minute at us. We only had one or two men killed and a gun knocked out and blown to bits by the time we were ready, so we lay down and smoked as it gradually got darker, and wondered what it was like to be blown to rags. By ones and twos we got to know, and then an H.E. exploded twenty of our shells

Pistol Gun

Told in the Huts

and another gun went west. Half the battery and two guns gone before we made a start. We could do nothing—no cover for miles—so I lay and smoked and wondered whether they had "Gold Flake" across the Styx or whether the only rations there would be "Woodbines." I began to get disgusted, especially when a bit of H.E. from Heaven knows where smashed my water-bottle, a decent aluminium one which I had bagged from a dead German "Kapitan." After a bit, ten o'clock came and we started firing. We did pretty well, and were afterwards told that we had knocked out several of the Bosche machine-guns, but not all. Meanwhile Fritz was not idle, and the stuff was screaming and banging all round us incessantly. Our shells were bursting only just in front, and the rifle and machine-gun fire was deafening. The air was absolutely solid with lead, steel and smoke, and flame and crashing roars as the big shells screamed over and burst. The ground rocked with the explosions, and the guns were dismounted time after time only to be shoved back red-hot into their places. Here and there we could see men in front and behind us showing up in the darkness against the fitful orange splashes of flame, and occasionally we would catch one as he flung up his hands and dropped, or stood swaying with his hand to his head, or wherever he had been hit. The gun crews were fast diminishing, and after a time I had all my work cut out to keep some of them from bleeding to death. One or two men were dead. The only N.C.O. left us was minus half his left hand, but cheerful. At 1.30 prompt the W. Kents and 14th Warwicks were creeping past us through the darkness. We lengthened our range, and then Hell was let loose in front of us. The shrapnel crashed and roared in the air and the Bosche machine-guns rattled, and in five minutes the two regiments were wiped out. A few survivors crawled back helping wounded men along to the rear, and the roar died down a bit.

The Ghastly Experience of a 2nd Lieutenant.

At 2 A.M. I was staggered by the arrival of a large party of fifty men with more shells, really intended for another battery which was now gone west—poor beggars! So the party had been sent on to us and had had only two men hit on the way. Of all the luck! We started off with three men to a gun, and I went out 100 yards in front to get better observation. I got a good corrector for each gun, and was about half-way back when I heard a shell coming. There was a great crash behind me, and I was hit everywhere and knocked flying on my face. My head sang like a telephone. I saw a regular blaze of green flame in front of my eyes, and——

* * * * * * *

It was daylight when I woke up, lying in a shell-hole with the wounded Corporal slitting my tunic and equipment off with a clasp-knife. My head was roughly bandaged, and I was a mass of blood from head to foot. My back was in "ribbons," as the Corporal said, and he added, "You ain't got no blood left, sir," and, he went on, "nor no left ear, either." This was greeting too cheerful, and I felt as if I would like to die at once and get it over. Clarke, one of the officers, came up to see how we were getting on—fortunately he had got some brandy, so I had a good gulp, and fainted. Clarke tried to find a stretcher for me, but they were all smashed, and the bearers dead. And still Fritz went on with his beastly guns. I heard Clarke and the Corporal say, "We must carry him, then." But I crawled to my feet and staggered round; only one gun was left, and all the wounded were dead or carried away by the shell-party. The next I remember was Clarke dragging me down into the valley towards "home." The shrapnel still roared over us, and I cried like a kid with sheer loss of nerve and terror. We stumbled over dead and dying men everywhere, and I

Told in the Huts.

bled on like a pig, as I crawled along on Clarke's arm. He dragged me down into Gun Valley and up the other side of Montauban, and a mile down the Fricourt Road we found an ambulance. Five minutes later Clarke was blown to atoms by a 5.9. H.E. shell. He was a good sort. An hour later I was in hospital and feeding. Then some morphia and to sleep. Just pleased to be out of it all alive—even if in rags.

East and West.

CORPORAL SMITH had a very mixed platoon. Men from Shoreditch mingled with men from the City who in the normal course of things would have been dashing about in frock coat and silk hat. Khaki has a wonderful way of levelling men up—or down—according to the point of view. The Corporal was a rough diamond, and liked the little authority conferred upon him by the stripes on his tunic. He was about to take the roll call :

" 'Shun ! Answer yer names."
" Wilkins."
" Here, sir."
" Jenkins."
" 'Ere, sir."
" Conway."
" He'ah."

Corporal Smith looked up, fixed a glassy eye on Conway from Threadneedle Street, and said,

" Look 'ere, my man, when you answers me, don't shout ' He'ah,' say ' 'Ere, sir.' But "—after a pause—" if you was to meet me in the street, that won't stop yer from asking me to 'ave a drink—we're on a level then."

F. L. S.

Gas Mask

REPULSING A FRONTAL ATTACK WITH RIFLE AND BAYONET.

"Rickety Bill."

By Joseph Hocking,

Author of "All for a Scrap of Paper," "Dearer than Life," "Tommy," etc.

"You wouldn't think much of him, would you, sir, if you had to judge him by his looks?"

"No-o," I said, hesitatingly.

"He ain't what you call a smart soldier, is he? Look at his chest. It's a mystery to me 'ow he came to pass the doctor; but I reckon as 'ow something went wrong with the tape when they measured him. He can't be more than thirty-four inches, and if you ask me, there's something wrong with his eyes."

"Can't he shoot straight?"

"Oh, 'e ain't a bad shot; but when he takes off 'is glasses you can't tell which way he's looking. As for drill, I tell you, sir, I never had such a job in my life as I had with him. 'Sergeant,' said he to me one evening after I'd given him a reg'lar good jawing, 'Sergeant, I've tried, and I've tried, but I can't get the grip of that formin' fours. It needs more brains than I've got to understand it.'"

"Still, you licked him into shape!"

"Licked him into shape! I tell you, sir—but there——!"

We were standing near the Water Tower in Ypres, which is one of the very few buildings which remained in

Sergeant Major

Told in the Huts.

that old historic city when I visited it in the winter of 1915. Near us was a tall, thin, shambling young fellow, who, as the Sergeant said, could not by any stretch of the imagination be called a smart soldier. Still, he interested me, and the Sergeant's remarks about him were elicited by my question as to who he was.

"His pals call him Rickety Bill—leastways, they did."

"Don't they now?"

"*No, sir!*"

"Why? Has he done anything special?"

"I'll tell you, sir. Between you and me, he had a drop too much beer when he joined, else I don't think he'd ever have had the pluck to do it. Fact is that was his trouble. He was on the booze whenever he had the chance. It's all on account of a girl, sir."

"In what way?"

"Nothing extraordinary. He's not the kind of chap a girl would go mad about, is he? Her name was Elsie May, and she was the prettiest little bit of fluff in the town where we was billeted. But she'd have nothing to say to him, although he tried, and tried. The truth was, she was sweet on Harry Dixon, and as you may say, she and Harry was engaged. He was a smart chap, was Harry, and good-looking, too.

"After a bit we got moved on to another place, and Bill got drunk so often that I thought he'd get kicked out of the Army. Then the Y.M.C.A. got hold of him. You know what the Y.M.C.A. has done for us soldiers, sir? Why—but there, if you don't, who should? One of the workers took a special interest in him. Got him to learn French, and then persuaded him to sign the pledge. After that they got him converted. I don't believe much in religion myself, sir, but I can't deny that it made a change in Bill. He bucked up tremendously afterwards, and learnt his drill like the rest. Then, I don't know how it came about, but

Protected Scout

"Rickety Bill."

Elsie May wrote a letter to Bill—just an encouraging letter, sir—and told him that he might expect to do great things if he kept straight."

"Do you mean to say," I asked, "that she threw over Harry Dixon, and gave Bill hope that he might get her?"

"No, sir, not that, although I believe Bill thought it meant that. By the Lord Harry, wasn't he gone on her! He'd a-done anything for that girl!"

"And were he and Harry friends?"

"Rather not. Harry kind of looked down on him, and laughed at him, and played tricks on him. I believe Harry was the hardest nut Bill had to crack in the way of his religion. I tell you, I've seen him look at Harry in such a way, that I knew he'd a-bin glad if the Boches sent a dum-dum bullet through his brain. In fact, he told me, after we got out here, that but for what the Y.M.C.A. chap told him, he'd a-killed Harry, and made out it was a Boche who did it.

"As I said just now, I'm not what you call a religious bloke, but Bill nearly convinced me. One night I heard him praying; he didn't know it, but I was close by. And what do you think he prayed for? He prayed that he might be able to love Harry, seeing as how he was commanded to love his enemies.

"Well, it was last May that we got sent out here to Wipers, the hottest hole on the British front. I tell you, sir, we've had a—that is, we've had a terrible time. Shells night and day. 'Wooly bears,' 'coal boxes,' and the whole boiling of it without rest. You see, the Boches swore they'd get Wipers. But they haven't got it yet!

"Last August—no, it was September, the Boches made a regular dead set on us. They bombarded us like—like—well, I can't find the right word, sir; but you can guess. It was very hot weather, and what with the smells, and the fighting it—it was the very—that is, it wasn't a picnic. It

Told in the Huts.

was a hand-to-hand job, sir, hour after hour, fighting, stabbing, killing.

"Then Harry, who was right in it, got it bad. A chest wound. He cried out for water he did, said his throat was burning. But we hadn't got no water. It had all been drunk hours before, and the fighting was so hot that none could be got to us.

"The doctor was holding Harry, and trying to do what he could for him, but Harry kept crying for water. Bill, who was close by, said, ' I can get water, sir.'

"'Where, my man?' asked the doctor.

"'There's a spring over yonder, sir, by that tree. Shall I go and get some?'

"'But it's right out in the open,' said the doctor, 'and you'll get potted.'

"'Water! Water!' Harry kept crying.

"Bill took his water-can and jumped out of the trench, and I saw him scoot across the open ground. He was carrying his can in his right hand, but he hadn't gone far 'fore he dropped it. A bullet had caught him. But he picked it up with his left hand, and went on again. We saw him dive into a sort of dip where the spring was, and a minute or two after, we saw him coming back. All the time the Boches were peppering him, but he still came on. Once he kind of doubled up, and I knew he'd been hit again, but he only stopped a minute, and then started staggering on towards us. When he'd got within twenty yards of the trench I thought he was going to fall, for he gave a sudden lurch. 'He's hit again,' I said to myself. And he was—in the thigh. But he still kept on, and then he just tumbled into the trench where we were.

"'How's Harry?' he kind of gasped as soon as he'd caught his breath.

"'I'm sorry to say he's dead,' said the doctor.

"Bill sort of gulped, then he said, ' Well, Harry'll know

"Rickety Bill."

—where—where—he's gone—that—that—I—did the best I could,' and then he just closed his eyes, and we thought he was dead.

"He was sent home to hospital, and he's only just come back," said the Sergeant, "but we don't call him Rickety Bill any more."

I was silent at this, and I don't mind admitting that there was a lump in my throat.

"Did he see Elsie?" I asked presently.

"I asked him that," said the Sergeant, "and he told me he'd never been near her. He thought it wouldn't be a sporting thing to do."

The Tables Turned.

At the Grosvenor Gardens Hut one evening a man in khaki was heard to ask one of the workers the name of the lady who had just served him with food. On being told it was Lady Ponsonby he replied, "I thought as much. Before the war I was a servant in her house, waiting at table. Now things are reversed, and her ladyship waits on me."

"Keep Your Head Well Down."

By a Sergeant in the Royal Fusiliers.

" Keep your head down, chummy, keep your nut well down,
When you're in the trenches keep your napper down ;
Bullets are a-flying, nasty bits of lead ;
It's all up with you, matey, if you stop one with your head.
Drills you through the temple, comes out of your crown,
If you want to see old ' Blighty '—keep your head well down.

" If the girls could only see me, they'd say, ' That's never him ! '
That is no Royal Fusilier, but a soldier made of tin.
Round-shouldered, looking humpty, with a back that's nearly bent,
But still I guess I can do my bit for the London regiment.
I don't care what the people say, it's a quidlet to a brown,
Old Fritz will never snipe me while I keep my head well down.

" I crawls into my ' Bivvy ' when my spell of duty's done,
Calls out for the Sergeant, but now I get no rum ;
So wringing wet and drowsy, it ain't no good to frown,
I gets beneath my blanket and keeps my head well down.
Take an old Sweat's tip, young chummy, if Corporal White or Brown
Is looking for fatigue men—keep your head well down ! "

A Novice in a Submarine.

A Personal Experience.

By E. Allison Burrows, A.S.A.A., Assistant-Paymaster, R.N.R.

Hearing this morning that the submarine lying alongside was to make a trip and a practice dive out of the harbour, I approached her skipper and made a humble request as to whether he would give me a passage or not. The consent was gracious and immediate, and with some feelings of excite-
... cabin to change into a dark uniform
he more or less spotless
e moment. At 9.30 a.m.
side an oil ship to fill up

ugh the conning-tower,
e uninitiated, one has to
e very akin to a funnel,
the passing of one's body.
l in which it is impossible
ining oneself against the
ks, dials, etc., which hang
ed into four compartments.
way wide enough to admit
Along the whole length
with the most amazing net-
simply gapes with opened-
s to be an expert mechanic.

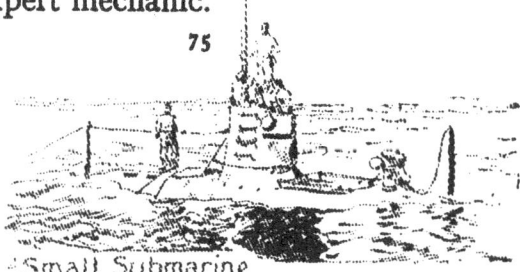
Small Submarine

Told in the Huts.

Mixed up are torpedo-tubes, pumps for pumping out the tanks, electric fans, cookers, warmers, indicators, compasses, a set of electric driving engines, in addition to the oil engines used for propulsion on the surface. On the top of it all comes the staggering realisation that here twenty-eight men and three officers eat, live, sleep, and work, and have done so for seven weeks on end without leaving the boat, cruising about in hostile waters with never a friendly ship or harbour in reach other than by a return down the narrow strip of water of a well-known Strait spoken of by all submarine folk as the " Hole."

The boat moves away with the gentle hum of a sewing-machine as she slowly gets under weigh, driven by her motors, practically no vibration being felt. The second hand of the submarine, a Lieutenant, R.N., now comes down to have a yarn, his duty for the moment being over. He explains with a detail which makes one's head reel, the uses of the various handles, switches, dials, engines, and what-not, that surround one. He shows me the bunk where the Captain sleeps, his own place—a sort of drawer which pulls out underneath the Captain's bunk, and the third officer's billet—a shut-up affair in another compartment where he sleeps with his feet on a torpedo-tube, his head on a motor, and with a torpedo to cuddle if the boat rolls. A decent-sized wardrobe, which on investigation turns out to be a wireless cabin complete, in which the operator—crouched like a monkey—can send and receive messages over miles of trackless space. The gyroscope compass is an innocent-looking piece of mechanism of which the second hand is particularly proud, although he curses having to clean it every day.

From a description of the machine he passes to a description of the previous day's outing, when it appears that by some mischance the boat went down nose first, shooting everybody forward and endangering their chance of ever returning. This is particularly cheering as you are on your

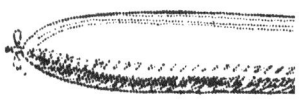

Torpedo

A Novice in a Submarine

way out to your first experience of diving in a submarine, and thoughts begin to creep in as to whether it is going to be quite as interesting as to make it worth while, and whether if you do happen to go to the bottom you will be found and rescued. But it is too late to turn back, as one cannot get out and walk.

During this time the submarine has been running on the surface and been navigated from the conning-tower. The order is now given, "Diving stations," and five or six men appear, coming down the funnel like so many big rats down a water-pipe, followed by the skipper. The men take up their stations at various wheels and indicators, the conning-tower hatch is closed, unintelligible orders are given, and ... nothing happens, at any rate so far as one's feelings are concerned. One knows the boat is submerging because one's eyes are on a dial which has been pointed out as indicating the depth to which the boat is submerged, and this indicator slowly travels from one, two, five, ten, fifteen, twenty, twenty-five, thirty feet, and you are "down under." "If anything happens now?" The thought gives one the feeling of a trapped rat, and the air seems to become suddenly warmer and vitiated. This is only nerves, however, and passes almost at once when an opportunity is given to look through the periscope at the world above.

There are two periscopes, and from the one the other can be seen sticking above the water a foot or so, making a ripple in the sea as the boat passes along. The surrounding hills and camps, the town, and shipping in the bay are all clearly visible, and immediately behind comes a torpedo-boat standing by in case of accident, as this is a trial dip to obtain the buoyancy of the boat after oiling. It is extremely difficult to realise that one is really underneath the surface, some 27 or 30 feet below the spot from which the eye of the periscope makes things visible.

Suddenly, as you gaze, your vision is obscured by a grey

Told in the Huts.

mist, then blackness ; the boat is deeper still, periscope and all being submerged. As the eye of the submarine comes up again, one spots a Dreadnought steaming into the harbour, huge, grey, and grim, but the submarine, with its wicked eye just peeping over the crest of the wavelets, is capable of sinking that proud monster and its thousand men in five minutes with one shot from her torpedo-tubes. As you watch, the water seems to recede from your eyes and you see apparently from some distance above, although in fact you are beneath them, the bows of the submarine emerge from the water. One is once more on the water-surface and in the world of things that breathe with lungs and have warm blood in their veins.

A deafening clatter strikes one's ears, which gives the impression that the whole boat is being hammered to pieces. One turns in alarm to see the grinning face of the second hand, who shouts in your ear, " Blowing out the tanks." The conning-tower hatch is now opened and one can go on deck and make the return journey in the fresh air and sunlight. Having now had the first experience of a submarine, the desire is for more, and that next time one may be privileged to see a torpedo-boat run, better still, something torpedoed, that is from the point of view of a submarine. One returns to the parent ship for lunch aghast with the marvels one has seen, and the biggest marvel of all, what kind of men are these who volunteer for such hardships and danger, whose home is a narrow steel tube filled with reverberating machinery and humming motors, surrounded by a waste of waters, cut off from all assistance if aught should befall.

A neutral ship being blown up by a loose mine

Wendersby the "Immortal."

By Bombardier G. H., R.G.A.

When the history of the war comes to be written it will be Lance-Corporal Wendersby who will figure most prominently in autobiographies and official accounts. From Ypres to Arras his name was a by-word—a magic talisman which set ears agog for the details of his latest exploit. Yet he was a modest man, so modest that it took eighteen months of time to convince him that his appellation of "Immortal" was justified.

He sprang from no great family nor benefited by no university education—in fact, he was nothing more glorious than a draper's assistant, which peace-time occupation doubtless assisted him to some extent in taking the correct measure of the enemy.

He commenced his actual war experiences in similar fashion to a million other men—in a filthy dug-out near the front line; then back to billets for forty-eight hours and up again.

Nothing happened during the first six months to brand him as anything other than normal, saving that he kept his skin wonderfully intact—a matter of no small difficulty when the daily gift from heaven is in the nature of scrap-iron and door handles.

After twelve months, when the original battalion was practically non-existent, and he constituted a fair proportion of what remained, people began to vote him "lucky dog."

 Told in the Huts.

Thinking this over in his dug-out, and working on the strange law of average, he came to the conclusion that he should have been dead three times already. This astounding discovery was a little disconcerting at first, but he kept his head and argued that his slimness was giving the law of average a knotty time.

It was when siege warfare gave place to sporadic infantry attacks that men began to regard him as uncanny. In every charge Wendersby was in the forefront whooping like a schoolboy, and disregarding cover with amazing recklessness—and yet he always came home, blithely whistling.

There is usually a limit to such extraordinary fortune, but the fates who dealt the cards to Athelstone Wendersby were lavish in their treatment—all the death-dealing, disfiguring steel and lead took a positive delight in passing him by.

The men began to whisper superstitiously and say he could not be killed. The day of his birth was noted and held as a sure emblem of immortality, till somebody discovered another man born exactly at the same time, who was carried away a week later. Thus all theorising was immediately stifled.

It was when he was hard up that he did the thing which got him seriously reprimanded by the Captain. Several men had fashioned a small cardboard target and were holding it above the trench on the point of a rifle. From the enemy trench, a hundred yards away, Fritz and his friends were "potting" at it. One crack shot had put two balls clean through the two-inch bull's-eye, to the admiration of its exhibitors.

"Say, matie," said a Lancashire lad to Wendersby, " I'll bet five bob thou doesn't get on th' trench top and tell yon sausage he's got two bull's-eyes."

In a moment Wendersby was scrambling up the parapet—a dozen hands tried to drag him down, but he knocked them

Wendersby the "Immortal."

away with a mad laugh and eventually stood fully exposed, jeering at the enemy trench.

"You can't hit me," he shouted, and executed a ridiculous kind of step-dance. There was a hum of bullets, but still he stood there and jeered until someone thrust a rifle-butt between his legs and brought him with a crash into his trench.

There was no doubt about it after that. He was the man who couldn't be hit—the beloved of the gods. In future he performed his scatter-brain tricks without fear of interruption, and men watched him clamber over the trench-side to do a bit of reconnoitring, knowing he would return—and return he always did, with a sniper, a pair of dead Hun's boots or some other marketable trophy.

There was no limit to his escapades. He would load himself with Mills' bombs, walk straight over to the enemy trench and scatter them, returning quite casually to describe the various effects.

Someone suggested that he should swallow a bayonet-blade, but he withered the quite serious admirer with a glance, for he took his gift of apparent immortality soberly, as if it were his due by some virtue of his parentage.

"Wendersby," said the Captain one day, "here's an urgent message. Run over with it to —— and be careful—don't get hit."

"No, sir," he replied, "I won't get hit, I never am, you know. They *did* try at first, but I think they have given it up now."

He delivered his message, was awarded his stripe, and subsequently thanked by the Colonel, for it proved to be a particularly dangerous piece of work.

"It's not my fault, you know, sir," he explained apologetically. "The bullets simply won't come near me."

After a time the consciousness of his inexplicable virtue seemed to worry him. He began to look at wounded

Told in the Huts.

men with an air of envy. To get wounded became an obsession.

"You lucky beggar," he confided to a wounded chum, "you're going back to "Blighty," and here am I till the thing's all over. And what then?—not a blessed wound or anything to show for my money."

"Never mind," was the reply; "you may have luck yet—you never know."

"No," he said sadly. "They'll never hit me. There must be something wrong with me somewhere. I believe I must have the transmigrated soul of one of those old Greek chaps that never died."

Then one morning a strange thing happened. Wendersby was out reconnoitring with a small party of men. They came upon a neat little wood that loomed suspiciously in the sunlight, and Wendersby left his small party and went forward to investigate. It was hot and close, so he handed his rifle to a private and strolled up the road.

Before he had gone fifty yards they saw a burly German step out from the wood and fire his rifle point blank at the "immortal" one.

There was a flash and a short cry, and Wendersby was on his back in the road. At sight of the other men the German took to his heels. Never was surprise so fully expressed in the faces of men. Here was the "immortal" hit and downed. Completely paralysed with astonishment, no one was able to move for a second or two—and then there was no need, for Wendersby picked himself up, brushed the dust from his coat, and coolly walked up to them.

"Look what the blighter's done to my cigarette case," he grumbled, and held the battered article before their eyes. Slowly the hand went out and opened his coat, and a dozen pairs of eyes scanned the grey shirt—not a speck of blood, not a scratch of any kind was to be seen.

Wendersby the "Immortal."

"Send him home on leave," said the Colonel, when the episode was narrated. "The man's a marvel."

So home went Wendersby for six days' glorious holiday.

* * * * * * *

It was a week later that the news reached the trenches.

"Have you heard," gasped a private, "Wendersby's dead?"

"What!"

"Yus—dead."

"Garn, 'e can't be killed—besides, 'e's on leave."

"Ask the Sergeant, then."

The Sergeant nodded his head sadly and unfolded the terrible tale. Wendersby, the "immortal," was resting in his native churchyard, dead from *German measles*.

Mine Searching

The Lonely Soldier.

Our Chef

THE following story was told to me by a chaplain friend, who vouches for its truth. A man of a certain regiment, just for fun, put an advertisement in a well-known weekly paper, saying that he was a lonely soldier, and begged for some letters. He did not lack correspondents. By one post nearly three hundred letters came for him! The already overburdened field post-office entered a protest, and the man found himself before his C.O., an officer not without a sense of humour. "Is it true that these three hundred letters came to you in answer to your advertisement?" The man was bound to admit the fact. "Then," said the C.O., "you must sit down now and write a reply to each of them, and put a penny stamp on each!" The advertisement was withdrawn!   H. G. H.

The Kit Store.

ONE day I was helping a man to put on his pack, and as he fastened his many buckles and put on his bayonet, trenching-tool, water-bottle, and the many other articles of his equipment, he said, in gentle protest, "Seems to me, mister, that a soldier is a man made to 'ang fings on!"

Flattering!

THE Y.M.C.A. in a certain camp had run short of coppers, and one of the workers was sent out to try and get some. He tried numerous places in vain, but was at last recommended to try the "wet canteen," which was opposite his own Hut! When he arrived at the canteen there was enough business being transacted to compel him to wait his turn. He was doing this as patiently as possible, when one man, who possessed a very bibulous face, looked up from his pint pot and, viewing our esteemed worker with suspicion, said, "Go to your own pub!"

The Phantom 'Plane.

By Levorno Sabatini.

When men have walked hand-in-hand with death, and have gazed into the depths of the great unknown, the materialistic tendencies acquired in the routine of their former walk in life gradually become subsidiary to spiritual forces, which grow more real as the former tendencies diminish. That may be the reason why men after their experience on the battle-field often come to respect that which they have previously scoffed at.

We were in the stiff fighting at —— in Flanders, and had cleared the enemy from the barricaded streets and houses until the whole village was occupied, and had further advanced about three hundred yards. On our left flank stood the battered tower of the old church, an emblem of peace in a world of war, and surrounding it was the little cemetery, dotted here and there with slanting tombstones, now considerably added to by lines of wooden crosses, marking the last resting-place of many a fallen hero, one being that of a well-known airman, who had rendered fine service to his country's cause, and who had eventually given his life for it. Adjoining the cemetery was the old-fashioned rectory, standing in the midst of a garden of shrubs and flowers, now neglected and scarred by the ravages of war.

Our company was ordered to hold this advanced position at all costs, while our comrades consolidated the ground won in the village behind us. We were all tired out after

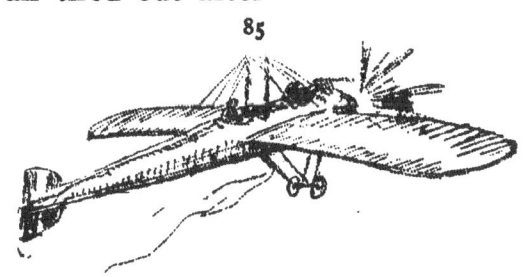

Told in the Huts.

much fighting and little food all day, but it was necessary to keep a sharp look-out for signs of the enemy's counter-attack. Meanwhile a heavy artillery duel proceeded, shells whizzing over us from both friend and foe, a "short one" occasionally falling very close. Our sentries were posted, and the remainder settled themselves for what rest they could snatch behind the existing cover, some lining a dry ditch, screened by a hedge, others taking the wall boundary of the cemetery, Jack Barton, a cool, level-headed man, being posted in the rectory with a machine-gun dominating the probable line of the enemy if they advanced. He explored the house with the aid of an electric torch, but found it deserted and empty, everything of use or value having been taken away, probably to furnish the Huns' dug-outs.

In the early grey hours of the morning, after a much appreciated rest, Jack signalled that the enemy were advancing towards us in strength; the information was passed on by field telephone to the village, and our artillery was at once increased to form a barrage. On came the first wave of grey-clad men, many falling as they reached the arc of fire, others pressing through it, a second and third wave following in rapid succession. We held our own fire, waiting for the enemy to converge across the fields to the road dominated by Barton's machine-gun. The minutes of tense waiting seemed hours, but nearer and nearer they came, not suspecting our presence, to within fifty yards of the rectory before Jack spoke with his "Lewis" and mowed them down like corn before the scythe. That was our cue, and before they could recover from the unexpected onslaught we poured rapid rifle fire in front and flank. Scattering like sheep, the enemy sought cover, leaving heaps of dead and wounded—a human barricade—in the roadway. Our respite was short, however, for they were quickly rallied and again advanced, though more cautiously, only to be

The Phantom 'Plane.

again repulsed. We were vastly outnumbered, and our ranks were sadly thinned as wave after wave of that human tide swept towards us. Again and again it ebbed and flowed, like waves on a rock-bound shore, and our position was rapidly becoming serious. It looked as if nothing but a miracle could save us and probably the village behind, though we fought desperately and sent back attack after attack. Reinforcements might come up, but only through a murderous curtain fire, for the enemy had grasped the position, and it was doubtful if help could arrive, or if we could retire.

A short lull ensued, during which the enemy seemed to be concentrating for a supreme effort. It was strongly attempted on front and flank, and it looked as if this time nothing could save us. Jack was working his gun with great effect; a glimpse of him at the window now and then showed that he had been wounded, for his head was bound by a stained white bandage. We held our fire, and with bayonets fixed waited the last charge, which we knew would overwhelm us. Thoughts flashed through our minds of childhood, of home, of dear ones, and many a silent prayer ascended. Perhaps those prayers were heard, for when things seemed hopeless and the enemy were madly charging with strafing shouts, to our astonishment there gradually emerged from the grey mists a great filmy, white 'plane, swiftly and silently advancing towards us, seemingly in a semi-transparent cloud, slightly luminous, but sufficient to instantly arrest attention of friend and foe. It seemed to be flying at a low altitude, but no obstacle obstructed its progress, trees fading *through* it, and showing dimly behind as they were passed. On it came from our left, flying just in front of the enemy front line, gently falling and rising with a rhythmic movement. Not a shot was fired, everyone stood spell-bound, gazing with bulging eyes at this supernatural apparition which appeared to be propelled by no human means. As it reached the

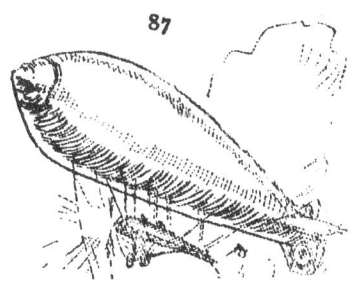

Told in the Huts.

extreme end of the enemy's right, it tremblingly halted as if taking observation, and then slowly returned, retraversed its path, and gradually faded away in the direction from which it had first appeared. Before it had gone half-way, however, the Huns had broken the spell, and with frightened shrieks of terror turned and fled in disorder. That is, all but their front rank, which stood with staring sight in the attitudes in which they were when first arrested by the phantom 'plane. There they stood, a long irregular line, across field and road, as if petrified. Whether they were killed by anything emitted from the 'plane, or whether they died from sheer fright at the mysterious apparition, we never discovered, and only a big round mound in the old village cemetery marks their last home.

As for our company, or rather the few survivors, we could not understand, but only accept our deliverance as due to direct providential intervention. We were shaken, silent, and awed. Neither afterwards did we care to discuss it except between ourselves, as is usually the case with those who have been in the valley of the shadows, and have gazed into the depths of the great unknown. Did the spirit of the airman, buried beneath that simple cross, come to our aid? We do not know, but we believe it as the most feasible explanation of the appearance of the "phantom 'plane."

Sleep Well.

By Miss N. L. Eley.

[The following verses, full of human pathos, concern particularly a young officer who, at the outbreak of war, was at Queens' College, Cambridge, and has since seen service in the Dardanelles, in Egypt, and in France. They also express the unspoken thought of many an anxious woman at home.—*Ed.*]

SLEEP well, dear brother!—here in your old room,
   A tender radiance, by the moon diffused,
A light serene, with kindly shadows blent,
   Is over all that you have loved and used—
Here—sombre books well thumbed by boyish hands,
   And prizes, hardly won thro' studious years,
Last season's bat, well oiled, your cap, your clothes—
   And on the walls I trace thro' mists of tears
Your treasur'd pictures, here some choice cartoon,
   Here mem'ries glad enshrined in those bright scenes
Of sport, and groups of boys—and there the card
   With pencilled cross to mark your room at " Queens'."
Oh, soldier boy! I lay my throbbing head
   Where yours has lain, while lips that tremble, spell
The prayer of faith—and whisper as of yore,
     " Good night, old boy, sleep well."

Tho' I have pray'd for every mother's son,
   On death-strewn field or on the awesome deep,
Tho' I have striv'n the common loss to share,
   And cared indeed for all who watch and weep—

Told in the Huts.

Yet now, just now—the severing ocean bears
   On its dark wave, one vessel, only one—
One precious freight more dear than all beside,
   And that, just you—my mother's youngest son!
Then sleep, sleep well—here in your old home room
   In all the old familiar places, prayer—
Unceasing prayer is wing'd above to Him
   Whose hand can shield you in that dread "Somewhere."
And if—here faith and fear in conflict meet,
   If you—so young, so beautiful to die,
Shall bravely make life's glowing sacrifice,
   And 'neath God's stars in that far loneness lie—
If this must be—oh, then—with honour crown'd,
   With peace which foe shall nevermore dispel,
And soul made white—until His great Réveille—
   Sleep well, dear boy, sleep well!

A neutral Ship

Peace Day.

By W. Pett Ridge.

Sergeant Ridpath—writing on letter-paper that bears for crest the red triangle with the familiar initials set across, and, below, "Canadian War Contingent Association with the Canadian Forces"—announced that he was coming to London on leave, and wanted one of the days to be a day of peace. He was good enough to ask me for suggestions.

I call for Sergeant Ridpath at what used to be known as the Horse Shoe Corner of Tottenham Court Road, but is now described as the Y.M.C.A. end. A brake stands there ready to take soldier visitors to inspect the notable sights of town; the intentions of Ridpath and myself are different. Across the way in Oxford Street we board a motor omnibus going west, and the Sergeant recognises that the clamorous traffic we go through is to be considered but as an overture to a quiet play. Just opposite Lancaster Gate in Bayswater Road we alight and enter the calm of Kensington Gardens. There, a stone-flagged space with water and flowers is Act I., Scene 1. A few nurses about, a few children whose deportment is almost too good to be true. A stroll southwards takes us to the statue of Peter Pan. South again, and there is the Round Pond where toy boats are sailing, and naval engagements take place that the Kiel Canal would like to imitate. Ridpath and I saunter through the gardens, and I am able to take him to Holland House. The grounds devote themselves mainly to the cultivation of tall grasses, but Ridpath has an acquaintance with the history of the place, and talks of Addison, who, by the ingenious device of marrying a Dowager Countess, became master of the establishment.

The Underground Railway conveys us from Kensington High Street to the Temple. (I ought to keep the Temple for the last Act, but London is a large stage and you have to do the best you can with it.) In the Temple, Ridpath notes Fountain Court, and thinks, I daresay, of Ruth Pinch and John Westlock; he sees the old church, Middle Temple Hall, the lawns, the quadrangles; observes, set up on doorways in large black capital letters, names which have long been known to him. We give an hour to the Temple. Up Chancery Lane, past the Record Office with its beautiful stretch of green, and to the right through Southampton Buildings, and on one side of Holborn is Gray's Inn, and on the other Staple Inn. Sergeant Ridpath could, I think, devote time to Staple Inn, with its quiet hush, and general air of a backwater near a turbulent river; and I, too, could stay, but that I want him to return a short distance, and rest in Lincoln's Inn Fields. The plane-trees in Lincoln's Inn Fields meet each other at the high branches, and give the shade of a cathedral; youngsters who sit about reading "Jasper Crump, or the World's Premier Detective," are engaged in the profession of the law at offices in one of the Inigo Jones houses near by, and doubtless reckon themselves to be in this way perfecting their legal equipment.

I have to apologise to Sergeant Ridpath for taking him across the clattering region of the Mansion House, and the Bank, and the Royal Exchange, but he has been in fighting near Thiepval, and he is accustomed to make his way through difficulties. Whatever there may be to forgive, is, I think, pardoned when he finds himself in an old-fashioned chop-house, up a narrow passage off Fenchurch Street. The luncheon hour is over, and the stress of mid-day traffic past;

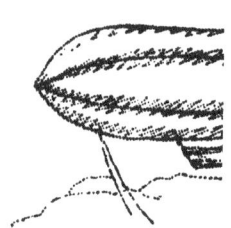

Peace Day.

Ridpath and I take a steak grilled as a steak should be grilled, potatoes in their khaki jackets, small squares of cabbage. Apple dumplings. (No one, said a friend of Charles Lamb, can have a pure mind who refuses apple dumplings.) Cheese and water-cress. The old waiter has the leisure to chat, and listens with respect to the Sergeant, but shows no tolerance for my opinions, preferring his own, and, if his statements be correct, with cause, for according to his statement he always said the Germans would be beaten if we gave our men the guns and shells; he never had any fear of Austria; he foretold to almost the very year the date when Rumania would come in. Happy the prophet who can look back and feel he has made no mistakes!

Ridpath and I visit one or two of the City churches: St. Benet's in Gracechurch Street, St. Katherine Cree, St. Stephen's in Walbrook. Ridpath likes them. He finds them soothing and restful. I happen to be in a position to conduct him over the hall and rooms of one of the City Companies.

"Sergeant," I say presently, "I'd like to take you to the East End."

"Sir," answers the Sergeant, accepting no responsibility, "you are the manager of this show."

We find off Mile End Road (breadth of which amazes the Sergeant) the Trinity Almshouses with courts and chapel, and the statue of Captain Henry Mudd, date 1696; also the Vintner's Almshouses. We make our way without hurry to Shadwell and to a churchyard at the river-side where the shipping can be seen, a thick forest of brown masts and a web of rigging, and children play at ball against the aged tombstone of Thomas Merwood, Master Mariner, who died on board the "Dowthorp" in the Gulf of St. Lawrence. Ridpath allows himself a smile of satisfaction when later, at the stone stairs not far off, I summon a waterman, who, once recovered from the astonishment of encountering a fare, agrees to row us across, and, after great manœuvring

Told in the Huts.

with the tide, and with big ship traffic, does row us across to the stairs that neighbour the Globe Pier. From Globe Pier, I know my way to Greenwich Park.

Sergeant Ridpath, sparing of compliments hitherto, gives praise to the view of the river and of the Hospital and Naval College to be secured from the hill on which the Observatory stands, admires the avenue that leads to the wide open space of Blackheath, enjoys his tea (taking his own time over it) on the lawn near the refreshment house, feeds the sparrows, estimates the ages of the trees. My apologies for inability, owing to suspension of the river service, to take him back to London Bridge by steamer are, he declares, unnecessary.

"You would not imagine it from what we have seen," says the Sergeant, in his deliberate manner, "but over there," with a jerk of the thumb, "over there, the other side of the water, there's a row going on. And I've got to get back to it. But I don't mind telling you I shall take with me thoughts of this peaceful day."

"Sergeant," I declare, with truth, "I wish you'd had the company of a more efficient guide."

And so home—after looking in at the old church of St. Alphege where one Major-General Wolfe was buried—so home by lullaby tram-car to the Embankment. Thence by Tube to the point already referred to as the Y.M.C.A. end of Tottenham Court Road.

[*Note.—The foregoing deals with the Y.M.C.A. system of Empire Guides, with its tours, etc., arranged for our wounded soldiers and men on leave.*—ED.]

The "Forty-Nine."

By Pte. A. H., H.A.C.

When Pte. Walter Firgrove kicked off his boots, flung his coat on to his mattress, lighted a cigarette viciously, and stuck his hands in his trousers pockets, it was obvious to the members of Hut 29 that he was " fed up."

"Look," said Firgrove, disgustedly, "here comes the rain again, and not a blessed thing to do from now till réveille."

"Shut up," said Micky; "your life's nothing less than a continuous grouse."

"I'm fed up," said Firgrove; "who wouldn't be fed up in a rotten hole like this? There's one man I want to see before I die, and that is the 'Johnny' who delights to quarter a London regiment in the wilds of Lancashire."

"Oh, Lord!" groaned a voice from the corner. "How long are we going to stay in this celestial spot?"

"Give it up," murmured another. "What kills my pig is the stopping of leave. What's the meaning of that?"

"Sheer cussedness."

"That's it. The Colonel's been away on the razzle for a fortnight. The Sergeant's had an addition to his family—I don't think—and worked a four days' pass. Every silly goat with a stripe on his arm manages to dodge off on some invented excuse, and we the backbone of the British Army——"

"Ha, ha!" laughed a voice.

Told in the Huts.

A great hobnailed boot rattled across the room and put an end to the hilarious interruption.

Slushby-cum-Chorburn was not in favour with the members of C Company. It was a mere handful of cottages, twelve miles removed from any large town, and plentifully devoid of any form of entertainment. On the marshes there were the usual eye-sores—trenches half filled with water, and bags of straw suspended from wooden railings, all jabbed to pieces with the thrusts of a thousand bayonets. Here a small portion of His Majesty's forces learned how to kill Germans in the most efficient and economical manner. None complained of the work, none complained of the Army generally, but all solemnly and religiously registered the conviction that Slushby-cum-Chorburn was the last place on *terra-firma* to be created, and, possibly through lack of material, was left unfinished.

"Micky," said Firgrove one morning, "there's a draft going away."

"Rot!"

"Fact. There's a crowd in the next hut going on leave. That's always a preliminary to a draft for France or somewhere."

"There's no draft," said Micky; "how can there be a draft when none of us have done any musketry yet?"

"Well, what's it all mean, then?"

It was certainly a mystery. So one man was detailed to go and make inquiries. He came back in a great state of excitement.

"It's young Swindell," he exclaimed; "he's got measles. Huts are to be disinfected, and all the rest have got fourteen days' leave."

"What!"

Astonishment knew no bounds. Later on, they saw the occupants of the next hut armed with grey slips of paper and grinning hugely.

Searching for Ideas

The "Forty-Nine."

"Ta-ta," they warbled to the envious ones of Hut 29; "sorry you can't come. What about 'The Empire' and that little grub-shop in Wardour Street? We'll send you on a few programmes."

"There's only one thing to do," said Firgrove an hour later; "one of you chaps has got to catch measles."

"Quite simple," retorted Micky; "*Je vous compriends*. I catch measles and you get fourteen days' leave. Quite charmed, I'm sure."

Firgrove furrowed his brows, endeavouring to find some way out of the difficulty. Someone had to catch measles, that was certain, and that someone must be recompensed, since he would not partake of the resultant fruits.

"I have it!" he cried suddenly. "There are fifty men in this hut. We each put one shilling in the hat and the man who gets measles first scoops the pool; come on, you blighters."

Everyone gasped. The idea was certainly ingenious, and forty-nine shillings profit was unanimously agreed as adequate recompense for the afflicted one. The shillings were dropped into the hat one by one, and finally locked up in a patent money-box.

Fourteen days passed and nothing happened. Each day members of Hut 29 were seen hanging around the portals of the disinfected hut, inhaling deep breaths through the key-holes and generally striving to become contaminated. Each evening and morning arms and legs were carefully examined for any sign of the familiar disease, but all to no purpose.

"You're a fine lot!" sneered Firgrove; "not one of you got the gumption to contract a few measle germs."

"What about you?" replied a voice; "you're no cleverer than we are."

"I don't want the wretched pimples," said Firgrove. "I want fourteen days' leave."

Told in the Huts.

"I don't want fourteen days' leave," said Micky; "I'm after forty-nine bob."

Another week passed, and still Hut 29 shone in the pink of health. The "fourteen-day-leavers" were getting visibly depressed, while several of the "measle-hunters" had already mortgaged part of the forty-nine shillings.

It was Micky who first found a promising trail. He had been to the village to buy notepaper in the little general shop that sold everything from string to cap-badges, and was engaged in conversation with the old lady who kept the shop when the village postman entered.

"How's the little bairn s'morning, ma'am?"

"Ah! poorly, poorly. These measles be a nasty thing. Poor mite is scratching herself to a shadow."

"What!" gasped Micky. "Has your little girl got measles?"

"Yes, and what with them and the housework and the shop to attend to, it's tired out I am to be sure."

He said no more, but went away to think it out. He didn't fancy the prospects of "scratching himself to death," but forty-nine shillings was a nice little sum, and besides, he could get leave as soon as the "stop" notice was taken off the "orders."

He made up his mind quickly, and on the following day bought a cheap doll and took it into the shop.

"May I see the little girl?" he inquired.

"Goodness, gracious! No!" said the old lady. "She has the disease right bad."

"But I've brought her a little present."

The woman's eyes softened.

"It's very kind of you, sir, but I daren't do it. What would the Sergeant say?"

"Oh, he'll never know, and I won't get very near to her."

After a brief argument, he won his point and entered

Camp's Copper

The "Forty-Nine."

Tea Pail

the sick room. The little girl was lying back with eyes closed and face swollen. He stood looking for a moment, and then the shop-bell rang and the woman left the room to attend to the summons. Now was his chance. He placed the doll near the pillow, stooped down, and deliberately kissed the inflamed eyes of the child.

* * * * * * *

"What have they built that big hut for?" growled Firgrove a week later. "Hope it's a new dining-hall. We want one bad enough."

"You bet it isn't," said another; "more likely a new mess for the N.C.O.'s. Just the sort of thing they would do."

No one noticed Micky rubbing his watery eyes and coughing dryly. He began to dress, then sat down wearily.

"There goes the 'quarter,'" said Firgrove; "we're all late. Micky, you'll 'do it in' this morning."

"I'm not going on parade this morning," said Micky. "I'm reporting sick."

The eyes of forty-nine men suddenly became riveted upon him.

"What?" said Firgrove, slowly.

"Sick, I tell you."

"Wha—what do you feel like?" asked Firgrove, with a wicked gleam in his eye.

"Mind your own business," snapped Micky.

After parade they doubled back to the hut, anxious to hear the doctor's diagnosis. Micky was not there, but an Orderly was standing surveying the interior blandly.

"Where's Micky?" gasped Firgrove, and then his eye fell on the shelf above his bed and he saw that *the money-box had disappeared*.

"Measles!" he muttered, "measles—he's got it—good old Micky!"

Told in the Huts.

"All you men sleep in this hut?" asked the Orderly, sweetly.

"Yes."

"Right. Get your kits and line up outside. Leave the beds and blankets."

Never was an order executed more promptly.

"Now, then, ' 'Shun '—from the right, number! Form fours! Left turn! Quick march!"

Off they went, whistling and filled with intense joy.

"Corporal," said Firgrove, "when do we get our passes?"

The Orderly raised his eyebrows.

"Passes, my lad! turn over and have another dream."

The forty-nine staggered in their tracks, and gazed at the speaker dumbfounded.

"Left wheel!"

They turned round the end hut and came full upon the brand new building. On its side was inscribed in nice new red paint—

"ISOLATION HUT."

"There you are, my lads," said the Orderly with a grin; "just finished this morning. Put your kits down, and two of you go to the Q.M.S. for new beds and blankets. Make yourself quite at home. You'll be all right here for about a month—ta-ta!"

THE ENEMY CRASHED TO THE EARTH IN A COLUMN OF FLAME AND SMOKE

The Seven Wonders of the Y.M.C.A. Hut World.

By Arthur K. Yapp.

Our Soloist

We were sitting round the stove in a Hospital Hut where the Y.M.C.A. was catering for the needs of men who had been sent there from all parts of the world. We had talked together of all sorts of topics, and the conversation turned to Y.M.C.A. Huts in various parts of the theatre of war. I asked the men what were the seven best Y.M.C.A.'s they had struck since the beginning of the war.

I.

McCraph, of the Royal Naval Division, said nothing he had seen could touch the Crystal Palace. He grew enthusiastic as he spoke of the great gallery crowded with men reading, writing letters, or talking to their friends; of the fruit counter and refreshment stall; the ladies ever bright and cheery, and the constant sense of hustle and "something doing."

II.

Smith, of the R.G.A., however, voted for Woolwich, where the Y.M.C.A. is established in many different centres, and the red triangle is displayed in the Drill Hall, over two or three clubs, three hostels, and several great Temperance Canteens—even within the forbidden gates of the Arsenal. Smith had been a munition worker before he joined the Army, and he had heard that twenty thousand munitioneers

Told in the Huts.

got their meals through the Y.M.C.A. every twenty-four hours. The titled ladies who served Woolwich, he considered worthy of all praise, and he voted the Drill Hall as the finest Hut going.

III.

"It's all very well for you chaps who have never been east of Suez," said Robinson, of the Blankshire Fusiliers, "to vote for the Huts here at home; but what price Egypt? There's no Hut anywhere doing half the good that's being done in Cairo. It would be almost impossible for a young chap to keep straight in a 'sink' like that but for the Huts, and of all the Huts commend me to the one in the Esbekia Gardens." His eyes shone with excitement as he spoke of the great Skating Rink with thousands of men in khaki gathering there night after night for music and recreation. "I don't know what I should have done but for the Hut," said he.

IV.

It was a big, burly Anzac who spoke next. "I know what the Huts mean to the boys in England, but you ought to see the Huts on Salisbury Plain! There are nearly fifty of them, and every one a home. Mud! yes, I should just think there is, but we forget the mud when we find ourselves comfortably settled down for the evening in one of the big Huts on Larkhill or Sling Plantation."

V.

It was another Anzac who continued: "You can talk about your Crystal Palace, or Esbekia Gardens, or the great

The Seven Wonders of the Y.M.C.A. Hut World.

Huts on Salisbury Plain; I know many of them and I love them all, but as long as I live I can never forget the tiny tent and the dug-out on Anzac. Under shell-fire night and day, in constant peril from 'Asiatic Annie,' we used to turn in there for a chat, for a feed, or to listen to the gramophone." As he spoke his eyes seemed to be attempting to peer into the distance; in thought he was far away on that lone spot on the Peninsula where so many of his comrades are sleeping their last earthly sleep. Once more he could hear the roar of " Asiatic Annie " and the rattle of the machine-guns, and the words of loving warning and good cheer he had so often heard in the dug-out on the shores of Anzac. With an effort he recalled himself. " Yes," said he, " the tiny Hut at Anzac was surely one of the seven wonders of the world."

VI.

O'Connor, a young Irishman belonging to the Munster Fusiliers, said the best thing he had struck since he joined the Army were the Station Huts of London. " Just fancy," he cried, " twelve of them open day and night! The last time I came back to 'Blighty' the 'leave train' was late, and I couldn't get a boat until the next day. I went to the Hut in Grosvenor Gardens, just outside Victoria Station, and never had a better sleep in my life, nor a better breakfast, begad! There were ladies to wait on us, too, and they did make us feel at home!"

VII.

Private Owens, of the Royal Welsh Fusiliers, then spoke up: " Indeed to goodness," he said, " you are all wrong whatever! The Huts in France, look you, take the cake!" It was a convincing story he had to tell. Early in the War

Told in the Huts.

he joined Kitchener's Army; went to training to Kinmel Park in North Wales, and there contracted the "Hut Habit." Later on, he was sent to one of the big camps in the South, and the habit became confirmed. He was sent to France, but owing to submarine trouble in the Channel was "held up" for a couple of days in Folkestone. There he found an enormous Hut under the sign of "The Red Triangle," and there he spent his time. Arrived in France, he was marched straight up to the Rest Camp, and there was one of his beloved Huts. He waxed eloquent as he told of the Hut at the base; up the line; at the railway station; in the hospitals and convalescent camps; how the men in the Huts organised games, ran concerts, lectures, and educational classes, and amid many difficulties did everything in their power to help the soldiers. "Look you," he said, "there is nothing to beat the Hut of France whatever!" And there was no reply.

The Atheist.

By George Goodchild.

When Private Reginald Conrad arrived in Room 8, C Block, with three blankets under his arm, kit-bag, haversack, bayonet, and belt, and such miscellaneous articles as basin and plate, knife, fork, and spoons distributed over his person, everyone gasped. For Room 8 was notoriously democratic, and Private R. C., with his lean, handsome face and gold pince-nez, was calculated to create a rather unwelcome discord.

"Blimey!" ejaculated Ginger.

"Strike me!" muttered 'Enery.

"Wotcher want?" demanded the remaining half-dozen.

Conrad dropped his load on to the floor and gazed around dreamily. Then he coolly took three planks from the corner of the room and arranged them neatly on the two short wooden supports. He spread the straw-packed mattress over these, placed the pillow at the top of it, and began to sort out his three blankets, carefully selecting the thinnest one for the bottommost position.

"I say!" said Ginger. "Oo sent yer 'ere?"

"Sergeant."

"Then 'e orter know better. This 'ere room won't 'old more'n eight."

"Why, there's ample room here, beneath the window."

"Yus—and wot abaht the rain—it comes in all through them there 'oles.'

Told in the Huts.

" Yes, obviously, and so does the air, thank goodness ! "

So Conrad established himself in the rat-infested confines of Block C, and the eight men—rough, uncouth, and hard-bitten—watched and wondered. They had never seen anyone like Conrad before. He never swore, never went out of barracks, but when the day's work was done fished from his kit-bag a worn and finger-marked volume of verse, and read on till " lights out " echoed over the square. Slim and ascetic of countenance, he amazed his companions by his physical energy at Swedish drill and on the long route marches under the burning sun with full kit. He never grumbled or cursed his fate; but sometimes, unconsciously, a look of pain and great loneliness came into his eyes, and the little book of verse would drop on to his knees, to lie there unseen by his half-closed eyes. It was Ginger who first held out the hand of sympathy.

It was on a morning when the postman yelled his familiar cry up the stairs and brought a hundred hustling, be-shirted warriors rushing like mad to get at him. All but Conrad had received something, a post card, a letter, a box of cigarettes. Ginger seemed specially blessed. In the midst of his delirious joy he saw the eyes of Conrad gazing strangely at the lucky recipients, and watched them move from man to man as though striving to analyse and understand the emotions which possessed them. Then it was that Ginger, in his rough, uncultured way, began to feel ashamed of himself. He walked up to Conrad, jabbing at the buttons of his coat with his " button stick " to hide his embarrassment.

" Say, chum, can't your folk write ? "

" What do you mean ? "

" Well, you cawn't say as they're dying to know all abart yer. You ain't had a line sin' you bin here."

" Perhaps there's a good reason."

Ginger breathed hard on a button, and stared.

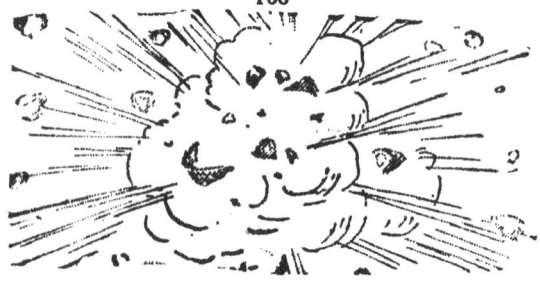

The Atheist.

" Perhaps there's no one to write ? "

" Wot abaht yer old man—beg pardon—I mean yer father, or mother ? "

" I haven't any father or mother."

" Well, sister, wife, sweet'art. You don't tell me you ain't got none of them ? "

" I do."

The eyes of Ginger narrowed a little, and one of his coat buttons seemed to demand considerable attention. He breathed on it hard, brushed it vigorously, and then mumbled something and walked away.

Two days later a miracle happened, there was actually a letter for Private Conrad. The address and the letter itself were abominably written, and Conrad wrinkled his brows with a puzzled smile as he read the contents:—

" DEAR CHUM,

" I hopes you likes your life in the army. Don't you think nobody don't care, coarse they does. I'll be always thinking of you and praying you'll come back all right.

" LIZA."

The letter caused Conrad an hour's steady thought. It was a crude joke someone had played on him—but who ? and why ? His eyes fell on a kit-bag, filled to the brim with the miscellaneous oddments which a soldier uses, and mechanically he read the owner's name printed on the side in irregular characters. There was something in the writing that was familiar to him. He turned to the letter again, and then realised that the same hand had written both; *and the kit-bag was Ginger's.*

He looked at Ginger, but Ginger seemed very occupied in putting on his putties for parade and steadfastly refused to meet the inquiring eye. Thus by a simple action was laid the first foundation of a friendship which was destined to grow and bloom and bear full fruit.

Told in the Huts.

It was on Sunday morning that Conrad caused a slight commotion. The company was lined up for Church Parade, and the Sergeant-Major was busily sorting out the various denominations—"Roman Catholics, Presbyterians, Wesleyans, fall out." A few men fell out to the rear and the remainder closed in to the left.

The Lieutenant arrived, buttoned his gloves, adjusted his sword, and walked between the ranks, passing an eagle-eye over buttons, bayonets, boots, cap-badges, and what-not, and generally making the company feel uncomfortable.

As he reached the file next to Conrad, the latter spoke up.

"If you please, sir, I wish to be excused from Church Parade."

"Eh?"

"I wish to be excused from Church Parade."

"Why didn't you fall out with the other denominations?" said the Sergeant-Major.

"I'm not a Roman Catholic or Presbyterian——"

"What are you?" inquired the Lieutenant.

"Nothing."

"An Atheist—eh?"

"No—call it an Individualist, an Agnostic."

The Sergeant-Major looked at the Lieutenant and then coughed.

"What's your name?" said the Lieutenant.

"Conrad, sir."

"Put him on fatigue, Sergeant-Major, this morning, and let him see the Major after parade."

For two hours Conrad slaved away scrubbing the grease off the benches and tables in the "Dining Hall," and then he waited on the Major. In most regiments, "Nothings" are ignored and counted as orthodox Christians, but the C.O. was a man of some soul and was interested in his men.

Conrad took two steps forward, clicked his heels, and saluted.

The Atheist.

"Ah, let me see—you're Conrad, aren't you?"

"Yes, sir."

"You have a conscientious objection to attending Church of England?"

"I have a conscientious objection to attending any church, sir."

"What are the grounds of your objection?"

"Religious belief, sir."

"How can you have any religious beliefs if you refuse to recognise the Church—and God?"

"I never said I refuse to recognise God."

"Doesn't it follow?"

"I don't see why one should make that deduction."

"What exactly do you believe in?"

"Man, sir."

"You believe in no Deity, then? How do you account for everything—nature, life, the universe?"

"I don't attempt to account for them, sir."

"But you must reason things out, instinctively. You can't believe that man is responsible for the heavens and the earth. There must be something behind all this."

"Yes, there is some governing, orderly force, but it may not be conscious. It may move and act, not of its own will, but in response to the unconscious consent of its correlative parts. Thus I may, unknown to myself, participate in willing the universe."

"You think you could unconsciously will and command something which is even beyond your comprehension.

"Yes."

"Why?"

"Because that infinitesimal point of all commanding knowledge which lies within each one of us acts in concert with its million kind. It is the inscrutable atom to which the fleshly vehicle is grafted. It survives death and time. It is the real man—the Truth—the imperishable and everlasting God."

The Pair

Told in the Huts.

The Major was a trifle staggered. He had imagined the interview would have lasted but a few minutes, during which time he would have converted the unbeliever to his own way of thinking. It was rather a blow to him.

"Then the gist of your argument is that man is God?" he resumed.

"Yes. The spirit that rules is scattered into a million million vehicles, and man is its most perfect vessel. It acts in the heavens and in the earth—in the tenderest flowers that bloom in the fields and meadows, but it acts as a whole."

"And you cannot believe that there is a conscious Deity beyond all this—One Who controls, and whose word is the law; One Who may exert at will external influence in our lives; to say yea or nay to man or woman, to crush or to exalt at His wish?"

"No, I cannot believe that," said Conrad firmly. "I live and move in response to my own will—that and no other."

"Very well," said the Major. "In future you can do fatigue instead of Church Parade."

"Thank you, sir."

II.

Two days later the Major accosted the Chaplain in the Mess.

"Oh, Armstrong," he remarked, "I've got a case for you."

The Chaplain looked over his glasses and smiled affably. "What is it now?"

"An Atheist."

"An Atheist! That sounds interesting. I must look at him. What's his name?"

"Conrad—C Block."

No record exists of the interview that followed, but it

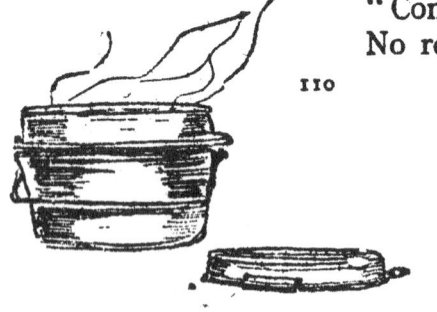

The Atheist.

lasted all the evening, and left the Chaplain in a hot perspiration, a little indignant, and not a little amazed.

"It's no use, Major," he confessed. "He had me in a dilemma because I could no more prove God than he could prove any of the fantastic theories he put forth. Unless one can feel God he ceases to exist, and that man has never felt Him yet; but he will do so. I am an older man than he is, and somehow I feel that God will reveal Himself in His own fashion."

"In the meantime, I have excused him Church Parade. It's no use sending a sceptic like that into a church against his will."

"Quite right, quite right," agreed the Chaplain. "A remarkable man, sir—a dreamer, and a great thinker, too."

Meanwhile Conrad went on with his work in his quiet way. Gradually he began to endear himself to the men in his room. There was a welcome absence of "superior airs" with him. He did more than his share of the work, occasionally insisting upon performing some thankless task because the man who should have done it was unwell or wanted particularly to go to town. He was unanimously voted a "sport," a real "toff." Only Ginger was silent in his admiration, and he so because he felt it beneath his dignity to appraise his idol. One summer evening, whilst walking in the fields whither he had been cajoled by Ginger, Conrad was astonished by a turn in the conversation.

"Say, Mister Conrad"—nothing would ever persuade Ginger to drop the "mister"—"everyone's a-sayin' you're an Atheist."

"Do they say that, Ginger?"

"Yes, they do—but what is an Atheist?"

"It's commonly supposed to be a person who doesn't believe in a Deity—that is, a God."

Ginger opened his keen black eyes very wide and stared—then whistled.

Told in the Huts.

" An' you don't believe in one ?
" No."
" Well, why don't you think there's a God ? "
" It would be unfair of me to tell you, Ginger, because—well, because it might prejudice you, and no man has a right to force his opinions down the throat of another. Every man must think for himself and find his own solution."
" But don't you believe all them things they tell yer in the Sunday school—you know, a 'eaven with marble steps—and angels with 'arps and things ? "
" No, not that sort of heaven, Ginger."
" Nor 'ell, with flames and devils and pitchforks ? "
" No, nor that either."

Conversation dwindled to a few casual remarks, and Ginger walked back to his room with furrowed brows.

On the following Sunday a second bomb-shell exploded on the parade ground.

Ginger fell out of the ranks and insisted upon seeing the Major—and see the Major he did.

" Well, my man, what's your complaint ? " inquired the Major.
" Want to be excused Church Parade, sir."
" And why ? "

Ginger fidgeted with the seam of his trousers.

" I'm—I'm an Atheist, sir."
" Oh, how long have you been an Atheist ? "
" Since yesterday, sir."
" Do you know that Atheists are very ignorant men ? "
" No, sir—Mr. Conrad's an Atheist—and 'e oughter know."
" Indeed ! And is it Conrad who has been putting you up to this ? "
" No, sir," indignantly ; " but if Mr. Conrad says there ain't no God, nor angels with crowns and 'ell with fire—*there ain't.*"

The Atheist.

"Very well," said the Major, curtly; "if you prefer sanitary fatigue to Church Parade, you can do it."

So Ginger was put on the filthiest and most unpleasant fatigue of all—but he whistled away blithely and didn't care.

Then the climax came on the following Sunday. Two more men from Room 8 pleaded Atheism, and were promptly "sat on" by the Major. Later, he called for the Sergeant-Major.

"Sergeant-Major, that man Conrad is a bad influence in the company. We must remove him."

"Yes, sir; but he would be an equally bad influence in any other company."

"Yes, I know. The best thing is to put him into the Signalling Class, and when he's passed his test we'll transfer him to another regiment."

"Very good, sir."

So Conrad was torn from the bosom of the circle that had learned to love him, put through a quick course of Morse signalling, and transferred from the 10th ——shires to a Siege Battery.

III.

The line was going forward. Everybody knew that. When thousands of guns have roared and obliterated the distant landscape for days on end, something lively is bound to happen ere long.

The Forward Observation Officer, with his battery signaller, wriggled like an eel through the long grass and tried vainly to whistle in harmony with the uproar. He found his station eventually, took out his glasses and peered over the high bank.

"Phew!" he whistled.

The signaller instantly became interested. He squatted down by the keyboard of his instrument and waited.

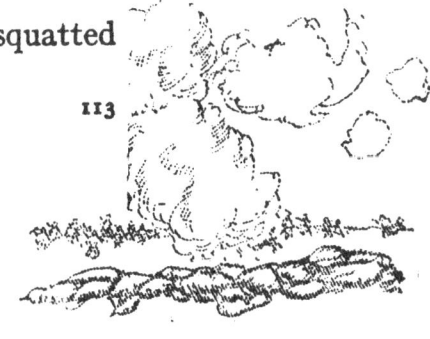

Told in the Huts.

"Tell 'em to rise 200, they're short."

The little instrument buzzed away like mad.

"What's your name?"

"Conrad, sir."

"Conrad, eh! You're a darned smart fellow. Play the piano?"

"No, sir—flute.'

"Oh, I thought so."

The F.O.O. took another look at the cloud of dust and smoke and became a little agitated.

"They're getting it. . . . No, still short, up another fifty."

The smoke shifted a little, affording him a clearer view of the objective.

"Great Scott!" he muttered, "there's a hundred yards of wire there, untouched. The men'll be over the top by 2.30. What time is it?"

He raised his wrist to look at his watch.

"Phut!" A bullet splintered the face of it and ricochetted against the wall of the dug-out.

He laughed a little grimly and turned to Conrad.

"Lie low—there's a sniper handy. What do you make it?"

"Two-ten, sir."

"Great Heavens! That wire must be cleared. Tell 'em to concentrate. What's wrong?"

Conrad was sending the "Calling up" signal, vainly waiting for the reply.

"Line's gone, sir.

The face of the officer became hard. He was sorry for the signaller just then. To "flag" the message, Conrad would be exposed to the fire of the sniper, with his telescopic sights, and scientific apparatus to aid him in his slaughter.

"I'm afraid you'll have to 'flag' it," he said with a smile.

"Very good, sir."

The Atheist.

In a few seconds Conrad was in the open, endeavouring to pick up a station.

"Phut! Ping!" came two bullets from the sniper.

"Keep moving, man," cried the F.O.O.; "keep moving, they'll read you all right."

So Conrad moved to and fro, "flag-wagging" for all he was worth while the F.O.O. searched in the distance with his glasses for an acknowledgment.

"Got 'em," he cried exultantly. "Now put it through, 'Commander 42nd Battery—very urgent.'"

The message went through to the distant signalling stations, and was telephoned still farther back to the huge siege battery.

The F.O.O. focussed his binoculars on the unbroken wire that sprawled before what once had been a neat little church, and waited. In a few minutes the expected happened. Barbed wire, steel girders, limbs, and earth were pounded to fragments. In a quarter of an hour that hundred yards of neat field-work was a smoking mass of ruin—a charnel-pit of unrecognisable remains.

"Lovely!" exclaimed the F.O.O. "George ought to get the V.C. Hullo, there they go!"

Unable to resist the temptation, Conrad crept forward beside the F.O.O. and looked down over the brim of the hill. Below him the British trenches stretched away in serpentine fashion into infinity. Out from them men were streaming in countless thousands. They made a rough formation, then, with bayonets fixed, went forward, mad in their enthusiasm. In the distance the smoke-cloud was slowly slipping away. Beyond that lay—what? No man knew, yet each seemed keen to find out.

"There go the 10th ——shires," cried the F.O.O. "A fine lot, that. Quick-trained, but fast goers—look at their pace!"

Conrad craned his neck forward. Somewhere in that

Told in the Huts.

mass of moving men were those he knew and loved. Somewhere there was Ginger. The thought of it brought a lump to his throat. He would have given anything for a sight of Ginger's hard, horny face, and a grip of his huge honest "paw."

"They'll have the devil's own time up there," said the F.O.O. "Fritz and his crowd——"

There was a shrieking of something in the air, an awful explosion, and Conrad was down with a sickening pain in his left shoulder. For a few moments he lay dazed and bewildered, and then realising what had happened, crawled among the mass of broken earth for the F.O.O. He found him eventually, half-buried in the debris, cruelly disfigured, and—dead.

For the first time a feeling, a great sickness came over him. It was so terribly sudden. A few moments ago he had been chatting in his good-natured way, pleased with his day's work—and now——

There was obviously nothing to be done, so he began to make a painful progress towards his unit.

The pain in his shoulder was getting worse, and his progress became snail-like. At the bottom of the hill he should have made a sharp turn to the left, but instead he entered a communication trench to the right and commenced to grope his way forward. Realising his mistake, he sat down and pondered over it. Why was he going away from his battery? Silly nonsense! Of course he must go back. He raised himself painfully and half turned round, then to his amazement he saw the figure of Ginger standing before him, beckoning. What on earth was Ginger doing there? He was about to ask him, when the figure disappeared round a bend; so he followed mechanically, and, turning the bend, saw the familiar form walking ahead.

"Ginger!" he gasped.

There was no response, so he followed as in a dream.

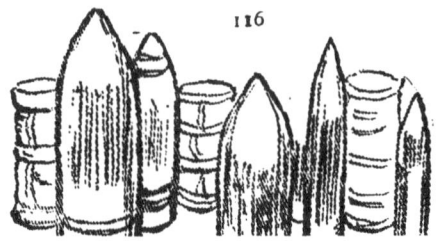

The Atheist.

Dinner Barracks

Through trenches, over torn, lacerated ground he followed his guide, his weary and aching brain never questioning the advisability or the purpose. On and on, over what was once the enemy's front line, until the gore and horror of battle was before his eyes. Stretcher-bearers were at work everywhere, but none seemed to see him or the man he followed.

For a time he missed his guide. He sat down and rested. Then he saw a water-bottle lying among the debris. His throat was aching with thirst. He picked up the bottle, shook it, and was about to drink, when his guide returned. He lowered the bottle to his side and followed mutely. At the side of a huge crater the figure stopped, and Conrad came up close to him.

"Ginger," he murmured.

The figure turned, and Conrad looked at the face. He stood speechless with fright. It was not Ginger at all, but the face of something he could not define. It was as though all the sweetness of life had been transformed into human visage. It held him breathless, spell-bound, paralysed with wonder.

Then, even as he looked, face and figure vanished before his eyes—and he was alone.

What could it mean? What was this figure that had lured him here? Was it a message for him alone—a message from—from—— He dare not utter the word, being filled with the sense of his own ignominy and ignorance. By the side of him was a torn cap. He looked inside—No. 28686, 10th ——shires. Then he began to dig into the heap of dirt at his side, almost forgetting his wound in his excitement. A pair of boots came slowly to his gaze, then a khaki uniform, and last of all a dear familiar face, pale as death—Ginger! There were bad wounds in the abdomen and a deep cut in the neck; the lips still moved nervelessly, and he thought they shaped the word "water." He held up the flask to the lips, and was gratified by the soft sigh that followed.

Told in the Huts.

Then he took the body over his " sound " shoulder and stumbled away.

* * * * * * *

They were lying in the base hospital, side by side, Conrad with a bandaged shoulder and Ginger swathed like a mummy.

"Say, Mister Conrad," confessed Ginger, "when you dug me out o' that there 'eap o' dirt, I just saw your face like as though it was a dream, and I thought for a minnit you was all wrong and that there was a 'eaven and we was in it—you and me."

"Perhaps I *was* wrong, Ginger," said Conrad, lamely.

"Not you. When I was laying there—seemed like ten years—not able to move a wink, I wanted a drink that there bad—so I thought I'd try a prayer. I tried one, but nothing happened, so I just reckoned there wasn't a God after all, or He'd have sent me that drink sure enough.

"S-sh," said Conrad, quickly.

"What's the matter, chum—bandages hurt?"

"No. See here, Ginger, you must never talk to me again like that. That drink you had—it was God's way of answering your prayer. Its purpose was twofold—I was merely the instrument."

Ginger opened his eyes with astonishment, then suddenly pulled the bed-clothes around him neatly.

" 'Ere's the Major," he whispered.

The C.O. came down the room with the Sister, passed a cheering word to the various cots, and eventually reached Conrad's bed.

"The Chaplain is celebrating Holy Communion to-morrow morning in the ward," he said, kindly. "Men who wish to take the Sacrament please give their names to the Sister."

The Atheist.

"You can put my name down, Sister," said Conrad, attempting to hide his blushes before the C.O.'s stare.

"Me, too," said Ginger, promptly.

"Well," said the Major, turning to Ginger, "this *is* a surprise."

"Well, if '*e* ses there's something in it, there is," Ginger retorted emphatically, stealing a glance at Conrad, "an' I should like to see the bloke what says there ain't," he added fiercely.

A light trench Gun for throwing bombs

The Red Cross and the Red Triangle.

By Lady Rodney.

When the war clouds first burst upon an over-civilised world in August, 1914, the foundations of modern life were shaken. The proud pillars of Christianity and progress were overthrown. It needed but the barbarous methods of modern warfare, as introduced by Germany, to complete the débâcle. To what purpose all the civilising processes of the last hundred years, the arts of peace, the piling-up of wealth and luxury—nay, even the long-fought-for altruism of social reform? Man was to be hurled back into the Middle Ages. Barbarian he was born, barbarian he would die: civilisation but a veneer on the surface of life, swiftly to be brushed aside by the elemental horrors of war.

Two organisations alone have sustained our faith in the steady progress of the human species, in spite of appalling reversions. The Red Cross and the Triangle proclaim the forward march, the steady evolution of life. Surely an act of lunacy, this slaughter on the battlefield! necessitating this loving salvage of human wrecks by the angels of the Red Cross—this re-building of the torn and lacerated body, this snatching of the dying out of the jaws of death! And yet here is the testimony of the modern mind to the sacredness of life in the body, and the triumph of mercy and love over hate and destruction; the perfection of science and surgery ever toiling to recover the lost. But the rescue of the wounded is nothing new: the utilitarian spirit of the past has always striven to save its man power—if only to fight again!

A Quiet Game

The Red Cross and the Red Triangle.

What shall we say then of the Red Triangle in this war? That is a new sign of man's deep need of physical, mental and spiritual support. Man is after all a spirit, and not, as Germany has expounded, a machine. In every camp in England, France, and the East, where British manhood has withstood this false Teuton ideal, the Triangle—the trinity of man's nature—has raised a living protest. Wooden huts, canteens, music, games, religious services, a ministering womanhood—these are the outward, visible sign of man's need of the humanities and the kindling fire of the spirit. The elemental courage and the robust endurance of an earlier age, man still shares with his ancestors, but the human and spiritual side of his nature has so developed that a righteous war needs the moral support of all that the Y.M.C.A. stands for, and all that the Triangle offers to the man at the front and the munition worker at home. Let it never be forgotten that the enemy is inflamed by the spirit of ambition, self-glory and hate, and the three are truly powerful levers. The wide-open doors of the Y.M.C.A. Huts, the incessant streams of khaki-clad soldiers, the peace of home in the camps of war, the loving service of the men and women who wait, the volume of song, sacred or profane, the letters home, the pipe of peace—all these human needs supplied, speak of the evolution of man and the steady growth of Christian ideals and values on our earth. Let us take heart of grace; should the whole gamut of civilisation be swept from the face of the globe, to be replaced by some finer structure in the future, the Red Cross and the Red Triangle will still be found among the relics of our age, and tell the tale of the triumph of spirit over matter in the great Armageddon.

Fresh Supplies

Drawn by Bert Wardle, Woodbridge Camp.

The place we wanted during the Crimea.

Your King and Country Need You.

THIS is a story told by a Tommy who is doing the work of a navvy—somewhere in England—and the charm of it lies in the fact that he felt no twinge of conscience in the telling of it. It was an experience which will be re-told for many and many a year, and who shall say that the details of it will not increase in their local colour as time passes on?

It happened during the last days of 1914, and during the earliest days of the war, when things were not as well organised as they are now, and we were often hard put to it to find a meal that was worth the trouble of sitting down to. If that is any excuse for what I am about to tell you—well, you must take it for what it is worth. But, when things go wrong with the British Army, it is not always fair to put all the blame upon Tommy's back. He has plenty to carry besides that.

You see, matters had been going from bad to worse in the matter of grub, and many of us learned for the first time what it was to go to sleep with an empty stomach—which is a poor bedfellow at the best of times. At first, there were only my pal, Bill, and myself, who did sly catering for each other, and we turned an old, deserted shed into a sort of private canteen, where we managed our own cooking with whatever came to hand. It was mostly potatoes and mangel-wurzels, which we pinched from the fields near the camp.

But there were seven of us, clubbing together, when we subscribed one bob a-head for an extra special Sunday dinner. Bill was the boy whom we trusted with the cash—with a full licence to lay it out to the best advantage—and off he started on the Saturday afternoon to the nearest town, feeling a rich man with seven silver shillings in his pocket to buy the grub.

Told in the Huts.

Now Bill was one of the best of fellows in every way, an all-round popular sort of lad, but he had one failing which brought him disaster on more occasions than this one. If he once put money into his pocket it was like pouring water into a sieve. Not that he spent the coin for himself, wasting it upon drinks and Woodbine cigarettes and stuff like that. He was so generous to his pals that the tinkle of the money against his legs was like voices, reminding him that if he had only two coppers playing with each other beside him, he was a rich man compared to the fellow who had none.

Well, to cut a long story short, Bill had not walked many yards away that afternoon when he overtook a lively party of the boys who were going in the same direction as himself, and we never knew what happened to our seven bob. But when Bill came back to camp that night you could have knocked him down with a feather, and he looked like a sick dog with a headache. The money—our money—was spent, and there was not so much as a twopenny bloater to show for it. If it had been anybody else but Bill there would have been some language heard that night, for we lads had been speculating all the afternoon upon how those precious seven bob could be spent with the best advantage to our Sunday appetites. But he looked so ashamed of himself that we had not the heart to swear at him, and I think our silence hurt him more than any words we could have spoken. We turned in hungry as usual that night, and tried to forget our disappointment in dreaming about that glorious meal which was to have been ours upon the next day.

Anyhow, Bill was not the sort of fellow to play a mean trick upon his pals, and he had evidently made up his mind that the special Sunday dinner was to be provided by fair means or foul, and none of us chaps guessed what was in the wind when we saw him busy searching for bits of wire and string in the ditch outside our tent. We thought he was

Your King and Country Need You.

avoiding us, and we all felt too sore about him to pay any attention to what he did.

It must have been sometime between midnight and dawn when Bill started upon his second expedition to provide that Sunday meal. He woke us all up when he returned, and we thought we were still dreaming when we saw a couple of plump young hens tucked, lifeless, under his arm. How he dodged the sentries is still a mystery to us, but he had the instinct of a hound and could see as well by night as by day. He was humming "Tipperary" under his breath, and the smile—which was seldom off his face—was wider than ever.

"Hullo, boys!" he laughed, as he held up the hens to our admiring, though sleepy, gaze; "what price your dinner now? My word, they are beauties, and they rose to my bait like a trout at a may-fly. This is what did the trick."

He took from his pocket a piece of wire, about a couple of yards long, at the end of which was a loop. This he deftly passed round the neck of the largest hen. Then he held it up for our inspection, while he addressed the bird with mock solemnity.

"Your King and Country need you," he said, as he gave a twist to the wire, "and you have to thank me for such a glorious death."

Then he turned to us with a merry twinkle in his eye.

"I thought I would pay a visit to the Manor Farm down yonder. Old Farmer Tippett has two sons there who ought to be in khaki, so I thought a fair exchange would be no robbery. I left a notice to that effect upon the wall of the fowl-house, which I hope will sharpen their wits a bit."

"What did you write?" asked I with some misgiving, for I knew what sort of a fellow Bill was.

"It was only a polite excuse for pinching the birds," he replied. "I wrote: 'Your King and Country need you.' I thought it would apply as well to the lads as it did to the hens."

The Same Thing—with a Difference

PATRIOTISM is an admirable trait in any man's character, though it may sometimes prove a stumbling-block in the way of expediency.

A Tommy, from the provinces, was paying his first visit to London and, during his wanders through the West End, he found himself in Pall Mall. Now, Tommy had a written list of instructions in his pocket, telling him exactly where to go and what to see. According to that paper, he was due to meet a friend in Piccadilly Circus exactly at twelve o'clock mid-day, when they were to adjourn to a certain restaurant in Soho for a meal at which Tommy was to be the guest. For reasons which were not entirely mercenary ones, he was most anxious to keep the appointment in proper time, but only ten minutes were wanting before the hour of the tryst. The thought which agitated his mind was this—How far was Pall Mall from Piccadilly Circus? Could he possibly reach the latter place at the appointed time? While he was debating the matter over with himself, he caught sight of a policeman, whom he at once accosted.

"Which is the nearest way to Piccadilly Circus?" asked our friend anxiously.

The burly representative of Law and Order pointed across the road.

"You turn up there into Duke Street, and then you take the first corner to the right into Jermyn Street, and then——"

But Tommy shook his head.

"Look here, Boss," he said, impatiently, "I am wearing the King's uniform, so there is no good trying to kid this boy. I ain't going down no blooming German street—not till I get to Berlin. Ain't there no short cut round by Buckingham Palace or the Tower of London?"

How Sergeant Juby Won the D.C.M.

By Levorno Sabatini.

Sergeant Juby was one of the old brigade. He had been in the Army ten years when war broke out, and was immediately dispatched to France with the handful of men destined to stem the devastating advance of the Hun on Paris. Many are the stories he can tell of that historic retreat from Mons, the backward march by day and night, when the little Army, outclassed in everything but their bull-dog courage, were pressed back and further back by hordes of men and weight of metal, to which they could make but a feeble reply; of the sudden, terrific onslaught which drove the enemy back to the Marne and von Kluck to despair, but that is beside the present story.

I met him at Liverpool Street Station, an excited hulk of animation, thew, and sinew, for he was going *home*—home unexpectedly and unexpected. His eyes glistened at the thought. In the carriage he was restless, the reaction of the tense life at the front, and the nerve-racking adventures of the firing line, worked him up to the same pitch of high hopes and expectation the schoolboy experiences after his first term.

The mud of the Somme was on his uniform and covered his heavy regulation boots, which had not been off his feet for nearly a week. It was honourable dirt.

"Have you brought any 'chats' home?" asked a chum.

"If I have," replied Juby, "they are 'honourable chats' —*honourable dirt and honourable 'chats'!*"

Told in the Huts.

In disconnected bits I wormed his story out of him, and linked them together. He had been in France two years and two months, and had only been home once. That was his only "grouse." He had been in the great push on the Somme for nearly a hundred days. "Over the top six times—*six charges*"—he shouted as the picture came back to him: "Compri? 'Mercy, kamarade, mercy!' they shout, when they see the glistening bayonets, but precious little mercy they got from the 18th ———. *We* did not squeal for mercy when they were driving us back; *they* did not show mercy to Belgium after they had crushed her; but it's 'Mercy, kamarade!' now, when the cold steel doubles them up before it gets near them. We took *our* gruel, and now they've got to take theirs. They are beaten—and know it!"

Then he told me how they took Thiepval in a grand charge after a killing artillery preparation, which left nothing standing and little alive; how they occupied and repaired the damaged trenches, and how he won the D.C.M.—and ten days' leave. There was dangerous work to be done in finding out the positions, locating batteries, and estimating the enemy's strength. One man might do it, where several might fail. Lieutenant Gilbey chose to do the work himself. Stealthily he crawled over, snaking to this bit of cover, then that, but ever making for a little rise from which to use his glasses more effectively. On he went, while the men, who would gladly have gone in his place, watched him in tense silence. On, slowly on to the little mound, through the barrage safely—when he collapsed in a heap.

"*He's hit!*" cried the men as they watched him struggle, and then lay helpless and still. "Who's going for him?" But before the answer could come, Sergeant Juby was over and away, zig-zagging swiftly in a low position towards his beloved fallen officer. By great luck he reached him, found him shot through both legs, and by greater luck—or call it providential assistance—brought him safely back; running

How Sergeant Juby Won the D.C.M.

the gauntlet of shrapnel and sniper, but only getting a graze on one hand.

The next morning he was ordered to appear before the O.C.

"Juby, you have done a very brave deed and have saved the life of a valuable officer. You will be recommended for the D.C.M. and ten days' special leave."

Juby clicked his heels together, saluted, and said, "Thank you, sir."

* * * * * *

"And now I am nearly home, boys, *home!* to see me dear little wife and bairns. Me little boy—so high—who can say 'Daddy!' Compri?"

BILL: "'Scuse me, sir, but c'd yer give me one of those 'ere Gippo fags of yourn?"

Sub: "Yes, here you are. But I thought you didn't like stinkadoras?"

Bill: "Neither do I, sir. But them skeeters is bitin' us somethin' orful, and we ain't got no more Keatin's!"

In a Garrison Town.

THE most noticeable feature of a Garrison Refreshment Hut is the apparently endless variety of its occupants. On one hand you may talk to a man who has taken Honours at Oxford, and on the other you will be compelled to listen to the coarse vernacular of the gutter. Yet you may find it difficult to pick out any one man from this mass of khaki figures. Only the voice betrays; the heavy ammunition boots and the badly fitting khaki have a tendency to crush personality. At one end of the room two men are singing a duet, "The Moon Has Raised Her Lamp Above," their voices blending astonishingly well in the thick tobacco-smoke. One or two men are playing darts and dominoes, while at the opposite end a bullet-headed little man is performing what he is pleased to term a step-dance, to the strains of a comb and a piece of paper.

Day by day I have watched these men at various forms of training, and wondered at the quiet way in which they live their new life. It is difficult to imagine that all this energy and action is devoted to one object—the taking of life. In the fields the signallers go through the Morse alphabet with flag, helio, and flapper. On the gun-platforms, men in canvas shoes take their stations around the great sombre guns, and the action of laying and firing is gone through solemnly, but marvellously quickly. In the parade ground infantry-men are perspiring in the hot sun, marching, bayonet fighting, jumping, hopping, and skipping. Out

In a Garrison Town.

from the harbour the squadron has just put to sea. Majestically they crossed the boom. The siren, but an hour ago, brought from the streets and houses thousands upon thousands of bronzed sailors, all agog with excitement—for a rumour has gone round, and the far-off boom of guns spells action. I watched them on their mighty ships gliding silently out past the fort, and heard the look-out man cry, " Eight battleships leaving harbour, sir." In the sunlight and opalescent blueness, seaplanes are flitting through the heat like huge dragon-flies, and beyond all this movement and spectromatic colouring, the smoke of factories goes up to heaven. Beneath the long array of gabled roofs one visualises grim, toil-worn, shirtless men ; furnaces and forge, hammer and anvil—sweat of a thousand brows and labour unceasing.

The man at the gun noticed these things too—it was obvious from the poise of his chin and the glint in his eye. He, too, saw the crowd by the pier watching the mammoth ships fade into the summer mist, mothers and children straining for a last glimpse of " Dad's " blue jumper. I wondered what the trend of his thoughts might be and those of the other men that traversed the gun-platforms or lived in the honey-combed recesses of the fort. Were they thinking of the hurry and scurry of the day, with its gun drill, aeroplane reconnoitres, of the thousands of men being transformed into soldiers, of the fighting ships steaming out to the unknown with decks cleared for action, and the thousand things that belong to war ?

Very soon I was to discover. In the Y.M.C.A. Hut I met him later, munching his bread and cheese and sipping his coffee.

" Something on to-night," I remarked.
" Looks like it," he replied in indifferent tones.
" Perhaps a ' scrap ' in the North Sea ! "
" May be ! "
He turned to a man behind him.

Posting Home

Told in the Huts.

"What time did you say that train reached Victoria, chum?"

His friend looked at a dirty piece of printed paper.

"Two-thirty."

"Ye gods!—then I shall be home at four!"

"It's a shame that those poor 'Jacks' had their leave cut short by the 'alarm'," I ventured.

For the first time he became enthusiastic.

"A downright shame," he agreed.

A few more remarks and I knew the trend of his thoughts and the prevailing topic of interest—it was "leave."

That was the question on everyone's lips—how to get leave quickly. These men had performed their day's work faithfully and unremittingly, and their minds swung as one to the theme that could never be forgotten—home. Fighting and working was a duty to be done, and done well, but home was the ever-present vision that ordered their lives. In ten minutes I had cajoled from him a little square print of a curly-headed girl with laughing lips and the eyes of an angel.

"That's my youngest," he confided—"sixteen months and a day."

Nearly all these men could have shown similar treasures, carefully stowed away from the vulgar gaze—a locket, a wisp of hair, and what not; and all the guns that ever roared were powerless to still such memories. At ten o'clock they filed out beneath the searchlight's glare to sleep and dream until the morrow.

A THRILLING CHARGE.

Home on Leave.

By "Ian Hay,"

Author of "The First Hundred Thousand," etc.

It is eight o'clock on a pouring wet night. Private McWearie has just gone on sentry duty. He is standing on the firing step, gazing morosely over the parapet and preparing for a damp and explosive evening.

To him, round a traverse, enters the Orderly Sergeant.

"You, McWearie," he says, "are warned for leave. The train departs at 5 a.m. to-morrow. Away to Headquarters and report at the Orderly Room for your pass!" He squelches away again.

That is the way leave usually comes—without any warning at all. Private McWearie pinches himself privately, finds he is awake, steps down, shoulders his pack, and ploughs mechanically through the mud to the reserve line trenches. Here he receives his leave-warrant and his arrears of pay. After that he is at liberty to find his way across perhaps ten miles of country as black as pitch and entirely unfamiliar to him, in search of a certain little wayside station which war has turned into a terminus. He arrives about midnight, soaked to the skin, but quite oblivious of the fact. His senses, being independent of such cumbrous things as railway trains, are six hundred miles ahead of him—at home already. He has four or five hours to wait. But he need not wait in the rain. Beside the station stands a long wooden Hut. Over the door is a red triangle and the magic letters "Y.M.C.A." These Huts have done a work in France

Told in the Huts.

for our soldiers which will never be forgotten so long as human gratitude counts for anything. Here he waits, in company with a still slightly dazed and incredulous throng, all afraid to blink for fear the dream should vanish.

About dawn—the hour of "stand-to" in another place—the train absorbs Private McWearie. Some hours later he is crossing the Channel, wishing fervently that he was back in the trenches. An hour or two later, himself again, he is standing on the platform at Victoria Station, surrounded by friendly strangers, who are anxious, firstly, to provide him with a free meal, and, secondly, to act as pilot to Euston. There is something very appealing to a tired man about the welcome at Victoria. The first time I came home on leave I felt quite ashamed at having to confess to a most masterful Boy Scout who wanted to take me in tow, firstly, that I only lived in London, and, secondly, that I knew the way to my own house. But did you see a picture in *Punch* not long ago of this very scene, with a raw-boned Highlander cautiously inquiring of a would-be guide if the station was far from the town? Can you see that man's own station and his own town? The town clinging grimly to the leeside of some wind-swept hill, while the station exists sternly apart on a railway which keeps to comfortable valleys and safe dividends.

Well, that man was Private McWearie. Next morning early his own railway put him down, with the mud of Flanders still encrusted upon him, at his own station. And here, with nothing but a two-mile tramp between him and his home, a truly happy warrior if ever there was one, I think we may take leave of him.

Destroyer

The Key to the Door.

A true sidelight upon the work of the Y.M.C.A. in France.

By Annie S. Swan.

Private Thomas Alderton was out of love with life.

It had rained persistently all day, and the mud was churning now under every step he took between the lines, in a Base Camp somewhere in France. A strange restlessness had driven him forth from the shelter he had shared for six weeks with thirty comrades, and to-morrow he would turn his back on it, perhaps for ever.

The great day had come, the moment for which he had longed and laboured was in sight, the object for which he had left his home and a safe, comfortable billet in Essex was within reach.

To-morrow he was going up the line. How did he feel about it? Frankly, he was not sure. Afraid? Perish the thought!

But beyond doubt there was a feeling of solemnity, a tense anticipation which had in it some element of apprehension, even of fear.

He was hail-fellow-well-met with his thirty comrades, a prime favourite because he always played the game, but as the day wore on he felt less and less inclined for the "beano" with which it was proposed to round up their last night at the Base. How was this strange reluctance to be accounted for in one who was the life and soul of every social gathering? None could sing a better comic song, or mimic

Told in the Huts.

more successfully, or so cleverly take off to the life those to whom outward respect had to be paid.

His absence from any gathering where he was known would be more than regrettable, it would be a calamity. But somehow as that last day in the Camp wore on, and the hour of the "beano" approached, he felt more and more disinclined to take part in it. As he came tumbling along the outer lane against the blinding rain driving in from the Channel, which rolled grey and turbid between him and England, he knew that he would have to answer the call. The night before, after the sing-song in the Y.M.C.A. Hut was over, the Leader had announced that a prayer-meeting and small service exclusively for the men going up the line on Thursday morning would be held in the Silence Room at six o'clock on Wednesday evening. It was Wednesday evening now, and twenty minutes to six. He would just have time to wash his face and hands, put on a pair of clean boots, and turn in. But he did not want to go. He was not religious, he had little use for the spiritual side of the Y.M.C.A. work. Like thousands more, he had sampled the Huts for the material comforts and the welcome so freely offered, and like thousands more he had been gradually won through them to higher things. He did not want to be won. He did not care for church services, or hymn-singing, or pi-jaw. He would rather live a short life and a merry one than a long one shorn of what he imagined joy and liberty, but which was really bondage. But to-morrow he was going up the line, he was one of those for whom the service was going to be held, and perhaps there might be a message for him. So many of those who went up the line never came down again, and Private Alderton had no sort of idea what happened to them except that they had been killed by a Jack Johnson, and found a soldier's grave.

But Mr. Carruthers always spoke as if there was something beyond this life, something above the noise and din of battle, some great reward which any man could make

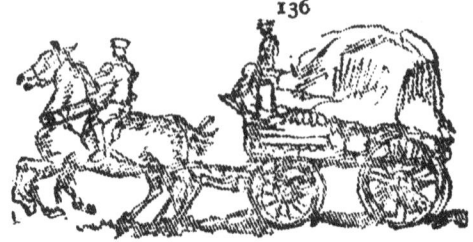

A Forage Wagon

The Key to the Door.

his own, for the asking, or the taking. When he made his way a little shamefacedly to the little Silence Room—not long added to the Hut accommodation—he was relieved to find that he was not the only one with that destination in view.

"Hulloa, Mac!" he said to a big Corporal of the H.L.I. "Goin' to the service?"

Trench Warfare.

"Ay," answered Mac, and they went in together. Already about sixty were present, and as the two slipped in near the door, they were immediately spotted by the Leader, who was already at the desk.

He was a slender young man of somewhat delicate appearance, with a clear-cut, rather pale face, and kind blue-grey eyes shaded by eye-glasses. His cross was that he was medically unfit for the fighting line, though he had three generations of fighting blood in his veins. He did not grizzle over it, but the men knew what he thought and felt about the war, and he had revealed to many hundreds who had passed through his hands what it actually stood for.

His business to-night was to prepare this handful for what they might encounter away from the safety of their Base, and when really face to face with the foe.

They sang one hymn together, the never-failing favourite, "Lead, kindly Light," then a brief prayer, and Carruthers was ready to speak. He used no book. Looking his brothers straightly in the face, leaning slightly towards them, his expression indicating how his heart yearned over them, he began to talk of the price which might be asked of them, and of the place where the full account would be rendered, and without the smallest mistake. In some such words as these he closed his brief and earnest appeal:

"To-morrow, comrades, you will be face to face with the reality, and Death will become to you a familiar friend, instead of a remote enemy to be feared and shunned. You may wonder at my choice of words, 'a familiar friend,' but I have done it purposely. We are met together here to-night to take off the trappings, and look the real issue squarely in the face. In order that justice and humanity and loving-kindness might not be altogether swept from the earth, you crossed the seas, pledged to fight for the right. And soon you will be faced with the ordeal of battle, called to redeem the individual and separate vows with which you entered the war. Some of you were not conscious of any vow; you joined because others joined, or because you felt yourselves driven by a force you could not set aside. That was the call from God, for King and Country, and you are going to meet the supreme ordeal in the same spirit in which you took on your training and prepared for the fight.

" Not all of you will come back, and my business to-night, brothers, is to assure you, with all the passion of a soul which ardently believes, that whatever the issue of the coming days, you need not concern yourselves. You are the sons of God, and He has you, living or dying, in His safe keeping.

" Further, this life is not the end and aim of your being, it is hardly even the beginning. It is but a stage. The wider life, the fuller activity, the larger room, where it will be possible for you to reach the full height of your manhood, is not here—it is on the other side beyond the hills of time, far beyond all the terror and the cruelty of war, as well as beyond its glory.

" You have, by so consecrating yourselves to the Great Cause, become entitled to an abundant entrance when the moment comes. Sons of God, brothers of Him Who made the supreme sacrifice in order that others might live, to-morrow, or any morrow, need have no terrors for you; living or dying you are safe. If there is any doubt in the mind or heart of any man here, I hope he will remain behind and talk to me. I cannot fight, all I can do is to try and help those who can."

The prayer which followed was punctuated by more than one sob, but when they stood up to sing " O God, our help

The Key to the Door.

in ages past, our hope for years to come," there was a light on every face.

When they began to scatter at the close, one or two lingered. Private Alderton watched the last one go, and then slipped back himself, for he was a shy man, and the thing he wished to speak of was new to him and he could not bear it to be touched upon in the presence even of a sympathetic comrade.

"Hulloa, Alderton, that you?" said the Leader, cheerily. "I was glad to see you come in. How are you feeling about to-morrow? Got plenty of pluck, I'm sure."

"I don't mind—it's what I come for, sir," answered Alderton. "Hope you'll excuse me, but I just thought I'd like to make sure that what you was sayin' a minnit ago was no fairy-tale. Honour bright, you *do* believe there's another life somewhere, that we don't go out like a bloomin' farthing rush-light?"

"Why no, Alderton, you must believe that! Think of your own splendid manhood. Would it please you to think or to believe that it would go down to the dust like the beasts that perish?"

"I haven't ever thought of it, but it do seem a bit of a waste. But if it's true what you say, it 'ud make a difference to the chaps what could believe it, make it more of an adventure than ever, so to speak. To-night 'ere, to-morrow there, so to speak. There's one thing I'd like to make sure of, that I'd see my old mother there. Do you think there'd be a chance?"

"Why surely! 'Blessed are the dead who die in the Lord.' She is waiting for you there, Alderton."

"Sure?"

"I could stake my soul on it—and I do," answered the Leader, confidently, and with kindling eyes.

"It's made it easier and plainer, thank you kindly, sir. I don't seem to mind now. I believe I 'ad a bit of a funk this

Told in the Huts.

afternoon. It's gone, and I don't think it'll come back. I'm ready for ' up the line.' "

Six weeks later, happening to be on the spot when a convoy came in at the Base, the Leader caught sight of Private Alderton, a cot case, being carried from the ambulance.

"Hulloa, Alderton! How are you, boy? Glad to see you back at the Base, even on a stretcher—not serious, I hope?"

"Dunno, sir, and don't much care," answered Alderton, smiling happily. "Come an' see me in 'orspital, won't yer? I want to tell you it was all true what you told me about the other side. My old mother, she come one night in the trenches and told me the same thing. Queer, isn't it, some of us this side, and some t'other, and nothing much between——"

His face was serene, and his eyes shining. Carruthers wrung his hand and hurried away with a full heart. He had had a trying and baffling day in the Hut, a day when everything seemed to go wrong, and lo, at eventide had come the bit of comfort which assured him his work was not in vain!

This is the work which is being done on every battle-front by the great institution of which Carruthers is but a typical unit. Who will help, for Christ's sake, so that our fighting men may be cheered and comforted and sent with sure and certain hope upon their way?

The Picket Patrol.

By Gunner L. T., R.G.A.

When you see half-a-dozen dejected-looking creatures in khaki with "frogs," and sometimes bayonets, moving at a funereal rate along the gutter, looking longingly at the heavens and hoping a kindly deluge will drive them into a "pub"—that is 'the Picket.

This morning I was "told off" with five others to undertake this delicate task. What I was expected to do I hadn't the remotest idea, beyond knowing that the business included the "clinking" of drunks and imparting a certain element of order in the khaki-congested streets. We scraped together a few bayonets between us of an antique pattern, about a yard long, and dated 1867. Horrible looking things they were too—dangling down below the knees, and threatening to trip up the wearer at every step. It looked like rain, and a discussion took place as to the advisability of wearing great coats, but the "No's" won, and we sallied forth and lined up outside the Fort. Then the bombardier arrived—half-an-hour late, wearing his great coat, and again the heated argument was revived. It was six men against a bombardier, and we won, despite his convictions that in a scrap a great coat is a distinct advantage. Firstly, because if one gets hit it hurts less; secondly, because it makes one look larger and consequently more frightful; and thirdly, because it is useful if carried on the arm as a kind of "thug" which one can throw over the head of an obstreperous "rough." All these weighty arguments fell on deaf ears, and we sniffed with contempt at the suggestion of possible trouble.

Told in the Huts.

Off Duty

Twice we circumnavigated the clock in the centre of the town, until a G.M.P. took us over—and then we commenced work.

The G.M.P. was Irish and appeared to have lived his whole life in the world of pickets. Every subterfuge which a picket may be guilty of was mere A.B.C. to him. He marched us down back passages where we could smoke, winked at every woman we passed, and generally conveyed the impression that while in the cradle his mother had crooned to him the ways of pickets.

Our chief job was to form a kind of human barrier across the approach to the railway station and to prevent any man in khaki from passing through it, unless he had a pass that would take him beyond a certain station.

Now when a town is thronged with countless thousands of soldiers, it is reasonable to expect that a certain percentage will resent the prevention of the very natural desire to see their visitors—chiefly wives—off by the train.

They rolled up in Companies, they bombarded us in Battalions, they came down the long straight street like a plague of locusts, and each seemed to have his wife and family in tow. It afforded us huge delight to see the incredulous look upon their faces when they were told that was the limit of their escort. Some of them raked out passes a month old—to try to prove they were *bona-fide* travellers, but we had an eye for dates, and politely referred them to the calendar. The sergeants were the worse. It seemed to them atrocious that a handful of stripeless men should dictate to them, and they became very rude. When a sergeant becomes rude he invariably resorts to Hindustani—it has, I believe, a wealth of expression not found in gentle Anglo-Saxon.

We made a special mark of sergeants, remembering the agonies we had suffered on parade—every dog has his day, and we had ours.

The Picket Patrol.

Then it rained, and all those sergeants and N.C.O.'s, who never die, stood and soaked and watched the train go out.

But it had its pathetic side. The next day a draft was leaving for the Front, and all the humour of the situation was swept aside by the agony of witnessing the kiss and the hand-clasp that might be the last in this life. Is it unmanly to confess to a great lump that rose in the throat and to a moistness that welled up from the eyes, unbidden, uncheckable? And the man—he could not hide his suffering, despite his magnificent courage. It was writ large in his eyes as he took his two "mites" to his breast and hugged them passionately, madly. I knew what he felt, for had I not dreamed of the day that might not lie far distant for me, and prayed that it might come quickly, that the misery of waiting might be shortened?

They were off at last—a jostling crowd thronging the carriage windows; waving hats and handkerchiefs, sobbing, laughing, and racked by a hundred emotions.

The G.M.P. watched the end of the guard's van disappearing round a bend, and winked enigmatically.

"Fall in, me lads!" he ordered.

We fell in, and we were treated to a dose of his amazing topography.

Never would I have believed that the town possessed such hovels. Back alleys, filthy narrow courts and squares, echoed beneath the regulation boots of the "Picket."

"Me bhoys," he confided, "for why should we be walkin' the shtreets? We'd be afther havin' thruble, an' it's a fool's game lookin' for it."

He turned and pointed to a bare-footed urchin who was giving an imitation of Charlie Chaplin.

"Toime he was aslape, the sphalpin. Hasn't seen a drap of whatter sin he was baptised for shure."

He led us by devious paths under a high wall, and then

Quarter-Master Sergeant

Told in the Huts.

we fathomed the chief reason for his strange wanderings. There was a nice little " pub " nestling in the twilight.

"Now, then," he warned; "thrae at a toime, and lave yer frogs and bay'nits with your chums."

We discarded our emblems of duty and silently slipped off. We had all refreshed ourselves before he returned, wiping his mouth and grinning hugely.

Back streets and alleys were traversed once more, and by a circuitous route we returned to the self-same spot— marvellously timed to five minutes before closing time. And then we issued out upon the street and found our trouble.

Four huge Australians were coming down the street, staggering and singing. Six yards from us one lost his equilibrium, and the other three promptly followed. Then it was our G.M.P. proved himself. He believed in evading trouble as far as possible, but once up against it, he was as he confessed *moutarde*.

Now Australians are big things to handle. They invariably depart from the set forms of horseplay and bring into effect extraordinary feats of thew and sinew. Our average fighting weight was twelve stone, and we had three bayonets, so we didn't care.

Seven pairs of hands shot out, and three Australians were in custody. Then there was an upheaval like an earthquake, a fearful clatter of boots on the cobbled streets, and the ball opened.

Something lashed out like a horse-kick and hit me in the solar plexus, and I saw a big giant of a fellow laughing madly and drunkenly. The G.M.P. took him on while I got my wind back, and then we all went at it together hammer and tongs.

The G.M.P. had a method of his own. He would frame up to his man in true pugilistic style and then dart out a long arm and collar him behind the knee and bring him to earth.

The Picket Patrol.

Two men were eventually taken to the Guard-room, leaving three of us to manage the big one. He was thoroughly enjoying himself, shouting out to an imaginary audience to watch his play.

"Just—hic—you watch me put him through the window," he hiccoughed, rushing at our smallest man, who was wearing glasses; and put him through the window he did, creating an infernal noise with the falling glass and his own mad shouts of triumph.

We got him at last, and frog-marched him till he confessed himself beaten.

It must have been an expensive evening for him! One plate-glass window, a pair of gold-rimmed pince-nez, plus the cost of the refreshment which had got him into fighting condition, to say nothing of ninety-six hours C.B.

Of course we arrived in barracks after the Y.M.C.A. Hut had closed, and not a drop of fresh water was to be had for love or money, but as the G.M.P. philosophically put it:

"You never can tell what'll happen in this place—drat them Australian's eyes. Heigho! it's all in a day's work—glory be."

An old Cobbler.

Drawn by Bert Wardle, R.A.M.C.

THE GREAT PUSH.

Concerts at the Front.

By Miss Lena Ashwell.

THE ancients symbolised war as a ravening beast—armies as fierce dogs unleashed from hell; but this, the greatest of all the wars the world has ever seen, is only comparable to a flood, a devastating flood that has submerged all landmarks under the waste of its wild waters. But even as the rocks remain unmoved by the fiercest storm waves and emerge unchanged when the tide ebbs, so underneath the tumult of war the immutable facts of human nature remain. And the Y.M.C.A. realised in the early days of the war that the needs of our men would include not only food and shells, guns and hospital stores, but some of the amenities of civilisation—food for the mind and spirit as well as for the body. It was when the war was six months old that the "Concerts at the Front" were started at the invitation of the Ladies' Auxiliary Committee, whose Chairman is H.H. Princess Victoria of Schleswig-Holstein.

In February, 1915, money was raised privately to send out a Concert Party to the Y.M.C.A. Huts at the Base Camps as an experiment. The troops were finding life under the conditions of modern warfare monotonous and boring; the hard work, an existence of rigid discipline in a sea of mud in a strange land, were enough to depress any but the irrepressible spirits of the British Army; and the rapturous welcome that greeted this first Concert Party was sufficient proof that some scheme for continuing the work was urgently needed.

Told in the Huts.

Out of that tentative beginning the scheme has grown to large proportions, and is continually increasing in response to the demands of all our gallant armies. First of all we arranged two Concert Parties to tour the Base Camps and the Military Hospitals simultaneously. These Concert Parties stay for three weeks or a month, and give about three concerts a day, sometimes to audiences of two hundred men in a hospital or to nearly two thousand in a hut or hangar. Then permission was received for a Concert Party of men to go right up to the firing line. Then Malta asked for a Concert Party: one was sent out there last winter and stayed six months, giving concerts every day in the camps, hospitals, transports, Y.M.C.A. Huts, and finally paying a visit of three weeks to that part of our Fleet which is in Mediterranean waters, giving a Concert on a different ship every day, to the intense delight of the Navy, which is even more cut off from home than the troops. This winter a Concert Party has gone to our splendid regiments in Egypt, and the Committee of St. John and the Red Cross Society has sent another Concert Party out to visit the sick and wounded at Malta.

The Concert Parties consist of six artistes as a rule—soprano, contralto, tenor, bass, violinist or 'cellist, and entertainer—often a conjuror or ventriloquist. But this August, by way of celebrating the tercentenary of Shakespeare and the centenary of Sheridan, we took a dramatic party to give scenes from "Macbeth" and "The School for Scandal," and modern one-act plays by Sir James Barrie and Miss Gertrude Jennings. We have only sent out good music, good literature; we find that nothing else is wanted—we only offer the best. The men do not want what is ugly or base, and it is difficult to make people at home realise how much what is beautiful and joyous means to the men who have literally nothing but the bare necessities of life—and death.

"You don't know what it means to us," is said to us over and over again by the men themselves, their officers

Some Conjuror

Concerts at the Front.

The Ventriloquist

and "padres." But we do know what it means to them when we see men standing in long queues outside the huts in the sleet and rain for hours waiting to get into the concerts, coming straight from a strenuous day's work and going without their supper rather than miss a performance of Shakespeare, crowding round the windows outside a hut that is over-full—nine deep to listen to what they can hear; and when in the hospitals we see white faces drawn with pain, tense with the awful memories of the horrors of a battle-field and the nerve shattering effects of our modern heavy artillery fire, relax into relief and laughter. They are never too ill to enjoy beautiful music or even to join in a favourite chorus song. When a nursing sister would have kept a " serious cases " ward quiet and undisturbed, the men asked that some music might come in to them. A dying man said to the violinist, " Give us something nippy, miss," and passed away as she played a happy tune.

The concerts are given anywhere—in huts and warehouses; in the summer by the roadside, in woods, or open fields; or in barns under heavy shell fire. A member of one of our Firing Line Parties wrote: " You will be sorry to hear that one of our huts near the line has been blown to pieces. We were singing there only a few nights before. The guns were very busy then. Can you imagine what it feels like to sing Handel's ' Largo ' to the sound of cannon? . . . We have been bombed in our billets, gassed, and shelled. What more can a fellow want? We are the happiest of Concert Parties."

Another letter from another Firing Line Concert Party says: " Yesterday we performed in a Trappist monastery which has been turned into a Rest Home. We played in the refectory to about four hundred officers and men from the trenches, all with that dreadful ' trench look ' in their eyes. But, glory be! We took it out for an hour and a half. Our reception was astounding. They went mad over

Told in the Huts.

every item—seized everything with rapture. I got them nearly hysterical with laughter, and the important Army Medical Officer in charge assured us that the beneficial effects of our performance on the patients would be enormous, and that the work we are doing is of *great military value.*"

As long as the war lasts, these Concert Parties must go out. The men regard them as a loving gift from those at home, a token that those for whom they are fighting and suffering, for whom they are enduring undreamed-of pain or discomfort, exiled from everything that life has hitherto held for them—that those at home do care, are with them, and are trying their best to help. The message brought back by one of our Concert Parties from a Senior Chaplain to the Forces is: "Tell all who sent you here that we bless them; if they only knew how much the music means to the men they would send Firing Line Concert Parties out in crowds."

But the letters that reach me at 36, Grosvenor Street, from the men themselves, in all branches of the Army, are the most touching evidence of their appreciation. A private, who had been in hospital wounded and returned to the Front the day after one of our Concerts, wrote: "We all agreed that we would go back to the trenches and fight all the better for the happy remembrance. . . . I was feeling rather lonely, not having anybody to write to me while I was out there; I began to feel I was fighting for no one until that cheery Party came along. I can even now fancy I hear the sweet notes of the violin." That boy went back to the trenches and was wounded four times and poisoned by gas. Another lad wrote to me that: "It just made all the difference going into the firing line with that music stirring one's heart." That is the keynote of many infinitely touching letters which we get from the men themselves—" that music just makes all the difference." So all who have helped and are helping by giving time and work and money to make this work possible, have the assurance that it is of tremendous importance and " of great military value."

Dead Beat

Adventures on the Peninsula.

BY A Y.M.C.A. LEADER.

I.

When that Shell Burst.

It was on December 10th that we first knew at Lancashire Landing what it meant that the German communications had got through to Turkey with the crumpling up of Serbia.

Up till then, the Asiatic Forts had thrown over any kind of old stuff that came to their hand (this was during the latter months of our occupation).

But on December 10th began a new kind of bombardment of V. and W. Beach, Lancashire Landing.

I was sitting in my dug-out in "High Street," half-way up the cliff-side, writing letters after lunch, when a shell fell into the water not twenty feet from one of our most important piers, forty feet below me, bursting with reverberations that echoed back from the cliff, and throwing up a great column of spray. Another followed in less than half a minute, which hit the base of the pier, throwing a dozen men flat, one of whom was killed.

For the first time I realised what funk-holes had been made for, and I betook myself forthwith to their ample shelter. There for twenty minutes a score or so of us crouched till the storm was over, and going back to my dug-out to finish my letter I was visited by a Chaplain, who

Told in the Huts.

asked me in a doleful voice whether he might do anything for me. I wondered at this kindness until he informed me that the Y.M.C.A. tent no longer existed. I fear I thought nothing about possible loss of life, all my thought was for the store of worldly goods which were all that the Y.M.C.A. and I possessed, whose precarious home was in that canvas tent.

Was it a piano and gramophone that would have been destroyed? If so, good-bye to concerts; or was it Nestle's Milk and Tinned Peaches that would have got the worst of the blow?

I covered a quarter of a mile up-hill from the sea in record time and found that luck had been with us. For the shell had fallen in such a way that only seats and boxes had been shattered. There was an interested crowd standing round picking up souvenirs, and there are certain things that a wise Y.M.C.A. Secretary (at any rate on the Peninsula) does not inquire into. I never dared enter upon my accounts the loss to the Y.M.C.A. in tinned fruit that day. Evidence of the risk men had run was upon the clothes of more than one who had been spattered by peach-juice when the shell burst. One can speak in an airy way, only three men were in the tent at the time, one of whom was a wounded man upon a stretcher. He was the wounded, but neither of the other two were touched, and fortunately neither his first nor his second wound were serious, and he was out of hospital in a day.

From that time on, no concert or any of our affairs went with quite the same swing, for we were in an exposed position, and while men were willing to do their job under fire and stick it, it was different coming at night to smoke the pipe of peace and comfort when shells were whistling over. In the middle of our best turns I have seen the tent empty in four seconds at the sound of a familiar approach, and an audience bend like a field of corn being cut by the reaping machine.

Adventures on the Peninsula.

II.

Handy Man—and Hero.

There was a man who used to visit our tent at Lancashire Landing, by the name of the Handy Man, because of his only stunt, a piece of poetry which he would recite daily (until he was stopped) with great dramatic effect.

There came a week when he failed to appear, and meeting him on the beach I asked him the cause, and he told me he was under arrest for insubordination and bad language to his superior officer, and was now out picking up paper, for in those days the beach was being pegged out with posts and barbed wire and the paths kept as neat as a provincial park.

The afternoon that I met him he was at the same job. A shell came over and burst almost under the noses of the front pair of horses of a limber waggon. The driver was thrown to the ground and the horses made off in terror up the slope, the waggon bumping ominously in shell-holes and in danger of turning over every minute.

The handy man forgot his shame, and with a man's courage and a master's skill gained control of those four horses and brought them back to the place where the man was still lying. An officer coming up at the moment sent him off for a stretcher. "I am under arrest," said he. "Then I take the responsibility of setting you free on the spot," he replied, "for your gallant conduct."

That night he was back again in the tent, a happier and a wiser man.

Told in the Huts.

III.

"Paraffin Oil."

I hope " Paraffin Oil " will forgive me if he ever sees these words. I cannot address him by his real name, for no one knows it. " Paraffin Oil " was his title to us every evening in the Y.M.C.A. Tent at Lancashire Landing. He got his name because of a song he used to sing, the hare-brained chorus of which was " Paraffin Oil." I can remember but one verse :

"They took us to Mudros,
        Paraffin Oil.
They took us to Mudros,
        Paraffin Oil.
They took us to Mudros, and we played at pitch and toss,
And we got the Victoria Cross,
        Paraffin Oil."

He had not a note of music anywhere about him, but give him a tune and he would stand up on the platform and reel off his rhyme without reason concerning the glorious achievements of the Y.M.C.A. or the bitterness of bully beef and biscuits in a way that kept all of us rocking, and made us forget our troubles.

How's this for one of his choruses? It was in the days when the "Goeben" threatened the Straits and "Queen Elizabeth" hung about as well : —

"A roaming in the gloaming when you're in the Dardanelles,
Awaiting for the 'Goeben' to come down to test her shells,
When she gets to Chenak, she will very soon come back,
When she hears that 'Lizzie's' roaming in the gloaming."

Adventures on the Peninsula

He first turned up on the night of my grand mistake. Many things had to go on nightly in that small stores tent on the top of the cliff in the early days of our work, before the ordnance had supplied us with better quarters and the electric light had been generously provided from the Ammunition Tunnel, sales at the small counter, a sing-song at the piano on the platform, reading and writing squeezed in anywhere on the roof, plank seats. Then, having found the need for hot cocoa and biscuits, I determined to have a shot at it. So we rigged up a plank counter on barrels half-way down the tent and a barrier. When word went round the beach of "hot cocoa" we were besieged that night as never before. All four orderlies were turning out two mugs for a penny and two biscuits for the same price; one man two mugs, no more, no less. I myself mounted on the counter keeping the queue straight, and it was at that unlucky moment that the word was passed to me that under cover of the crowd my precious store of tinned fruit was being opened. Show no horror, gentle reader, at such slight occurrences. Accidents will happen in the best regulated boards. Show more horror rather that I lost my wool and lectured a crowd of cold and hungry men to the effect that no more cocoa could be served that night, that if, when the Y.M.C.A. was conducting its humane work, its property was not secure, and if they could not wait to pay for luxuries, etc., etc.

That was my grand mistake, for before me was a crowd of men who did not intend to be gainsaid. I stood my ground and they stood theirs, but the crisis came when I found that the whole tent began to heave ominously, and having regained my sense of humour and temper we returned to the work of selling cocoa.

And it was while this little incident was in progress that "Paraffin Oil" for the first time was appearing upon the platform at the other end of the room and keeping an audience in roars of laughter. It was only later that we learned to

Told in the Huts.

become familiar enough with the chorus of the catchy song he was singing for us to roar it with him :—

> "Then good-bye to the bricks and mortar,
>   Farewell to the dirty loine,
>   Hurrah for the planks and gangways,
>   And away for the winter time.
>   For the big ship 'Billy Ragamuffian,'
>   Is lying on the quay,
>   When the shovels and the picks,
>   And the Paddys and the Micks
>   Are bound for Gallipoli."

The last time I saw him was early one morning, dirty, unshaven, eyes red and sleepless, with a smear of blood across his temple, for during the night a shell had entered ——— Canteen, of which he and his mate were in charge, and he alone was there to attend to his badly shattered companion.

Laying Moorings for Battleships

Comradeship.

By the Right Hon. G. W. E. Russell.

"Don't let reformers of any sort think that they are going really to lay hold of the working boys and young men of England by any educational grapnel whatever which hasn't some *bonâ fide* equivalent for the games of the old country 'Veast' in it; something to put in the place of the backswording and wrestling and racing; something to try the muscles of men's bodies and the endurance of their hearts, and to make them rejoice in their strength. In all the new-fangled, comprehensive plans which I see, this is all left out; and the consequence is that your great Mechanics' Institutes end in intellectual priggism, and your Christian Young Men's Societies in religious Pharisaism. Life isn't all beer and skittles; but beer and skittles, or something better of the same sort, must form a good part of every Englishman's education."

Do my readers recognise the quotation? It comes from "Tom Brown's Schooldays," and from a part of that book which is too generally overlooked—the description of life in the Vale of White Horse, and the village feast, or "Veast," with its annual merry-making.

Great is the power of a popular writer, especially in the case of a young reader; and I must confess that Hughes's casual word about "Christian Young Men's Societies" and "Religious Pharisaism" made a dent on my mind which it took a good many years to obliterate. The book was published in 1857, and till the present century was well

Told in the Huts.

advanced my notions of Christian Young Men's Societies were coloured by what I had read for the first time in 1862.

I do not know whether Hughes (who died in 1896) ever came across the Young Men's Christian Association in actual working. I hope he did; for, though perhaps he would not have admitted that his words were incorrect when they were written, I feel certain that he would have rejoiced to know that they were true no longer. Indeed, I think he might have claimed the present attitude of the Y.M.C.A. towards athletics and recreation generally as a result, though perhaps indirect, of this social teaching. My own attention was first directed to the Y.M.C.A. by the experience of a young fellow who had been one of my servants, and who abandoned domestic service to become a professional cricketer. He was engaged by a famous county, and was quartered, amid very uncongenial surroundings, in a town peculiarly rife with moral temptations to a pleasure-loving lad. Some months afterwards he came up to see me. Rather to my surprise, he told me that he had joined the Y.M.C.A. The advantage, he said, was great. When cricketing was over, he now had some occupation for his evenings. He was no longer obliged to spend them in a dingy lodging-house, or to wander aimlessly about the streets. He could turn in at the sign of the Red Triangle, and there " you're always sure of meeting a decent set of fellows." The words struck me, as coming from a peculiarly un-canting lad, and as showing the real refuge from moral perils which the Y.M.C.A. affords.

My interest, once aroused, was intensified by what I heard of the Y.M.C.A. in the opening stages of the war, and I can best epitomise my sense of its value by saying that it affords its members the immense boon of good comradeship. I lay stress on the word " good." Comradeship is a necessity of a young man's life, but its influence may be a blessing or a curse. By good comradeship I mean comradeship as it exists between two whose faces are " set Zionwards "—who have

Tommy's Home

Comradeship.

the same fundamental notions about faith and duty—although they have attained to very different stages of Christian progress. Indeed, absolute equality of spiritual attainment is unusual; and the stronger brother may be an immense blessing to the weaker—not sermonising or dictating, but guiding by good example and warning against unsuspected perils.

The Padre

With a really good comrade you cannot go where you would be ashamed for your mother and sister to see you. You cannot, for example, go to a wicked play. And supposing that your friend is younger and weaker than yourself, your comradeship may prove his salvation. You can counsel him how *not* to spend his evenings when work is slack and he is looking round for some new amusement. At all hours, and whatever be your recreation—boating, football, cricket, cycling, golf—the same truth applies to all—that good comradeship will double your enjoyment and will also help you to repel the unwelcome advances of men who profess to be friendly, but from whom your conscience naturally recoils.

But the most sacred and binding of all comradeships is comradeship in religion. I should be the last man in the world to recommend frequent talking about religious experiences. An excellent clergyman whom I remember, in my youth used to say: "It is true that you must put off the Old Man, but there is no corresponding obligation to put on the Old Woman." But religious comradeship between two like-minded fellows might mean prayer *with* one another; certainly prayer *for* one another, perhaps Bible-reading together; for such as know enough Greek, an hour on Sunday spent over the Greek Testament; going together to some favourite church; above all, joint participation in the Holy Sacrament of the Lord's Supper. From the Lord's Table you will return together to your ordinary work and recreation bound closer to each other by the bond which binds you to the Lord. You will remember that your fellow-men who have knelt beside

Told in the Huts.

you, even the poorest and the most ignorant, should be no longer strangers, but brethren, with a definite claim on your sympathy and help. This is comradeship at its highest and best; and it carries our hearts forward to that glorious, and perhaps not distant, day which shall knit together the redeemed in everlasting fellowship and communion before the Throne of God.

a Zep sighted

"Earwig."

BY RIFLEMAN X., RIFLE BRIGADE.

NOTHING has done more to reveal the better side of men's natures than the great struggle through which we are now passing. I have to thank the war for much—including two missing fingers and a perforated lung—for it was the war which made me acquainted with the best man I have ever met. We called him "Earwig," for what reason I have not the faintest idea, but "Earwig" he was when first I met him, and as "Earwig" he will always remain in my memory.

I was drafted into a signalling school from a large Infantry Regiment, and there I met him in all his joy and mirthfulness. The camp was pitched on a high hill, and when it rained we moved about in rivers of mud; when it blew, tents were flung about like straws. There was no town for miles, and the work of the day went far into the evening. Life was a strenuous thing, and monotony a constant visitor. But for "Earwig" I might have been driven to a lunatic asylum, for "all work and no play makes Jack a dull boy." But "Earwig"—God bless him!—was the light of our existence. Never a night went by but he had some prank to perpetrate upon us, and seldom did he fail to remove the sorrow from our souls. It was he who organised everything, from concerts to sports, and it was he who gathered the boys around to relate some side-splitting joke when it seemed that a smile was impossible.

He would take any man's "Guard" or "Fatigue" rather than that man should be prevented from seeing his

Told in the Huts.

wife or sweetheart. I'm sure he never knew how much we loved him, for any demonstrative emotion is "taboo" in the Army.

He was not much to look at, being below the medium height and rather flat in the chest, but there was something in his eyes which revealed the sterling goodness of his heart.

Occasionally he would get a pass home, and then how we missed him! and moped about camp till he returned with his bright smile and his "Here we are again, boys!"

He was never meant for signalling, no more was I, so we conspired together and managed to get sent back to our regiment as plain riflemen.

I shall never forget the ovation of that day. His old friends welcomed him back with genuine delight, and I could see a moistness round his eyes as he grasped one by one the hundred hands that were held out to him. Always he was the same old "Earwig," up in the morning with a gay song, and buzzing round barracks like one of the joy-burdened things of the summer fields.

I have never known a being so filled with glorious life and so keen to distribute happiness to every man he came in contact with.

Not only was he the soul of honesty and kindness, but he seemed to embody the spirit of fun. Once he came into the recreation-room, and taking two white billiard balls from his pocket placed them carefully on the billiard table. Everyone looked at him curiously.

"Now then, boys," he said, seriously, "I've just learned a new shot. See that!" He placed one of the balls near the centre pocket and the other about a yard away in such a position as to offer a very simple "in off" shot.

"Now, that's a very difficult shot," he remarked, cocking his eyes round the company.

"Get out!" cried a dozen voices. "It's easy!"

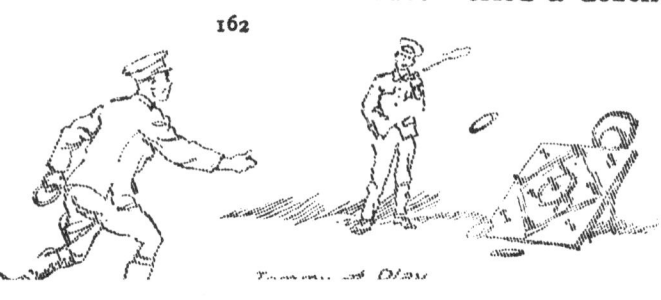

"Earwig."

He nodded his head slowly.

"Oh, is it? Well, I'm willing to give two bob to any chap who can get 'in off' first shot."

There was a rush to the table, but he kept back the throng, and beckoned to one man who was considered a good billiard player.

"Now then, Mike, you think you can do it?"

"I don't *think*," replied Mike, scathingly. "I could do a shot like that in the cradle."

He took the cue that was offered him, cleared a space for his elbow, and played the ball. A perfect roar went up as the ball "cannoned" and bounced away from the open pocket—*they were made of rubber and painted!*

Dear old "Earwig"! It was only another of his endless jokes, and by such things he endeared himself to us.

Then came the day when we sailed from Southampton, bound for the inferno that awaited us. But we didn't care so long as "Earwig" came too.

Those who have never been "out there" can never imagine what the real thing is like. All your vivid word pictures and feats of the pen can never "do" the thing as it really is. It was winter when we arrived, and it was early in the campaign when we were "sträfed" unmercifully day and night, and could make no adequate reply. We changed in those days, and wore the haggard look that comes of infinite suffering and close acquaintance with Death. But "Earwig" never changed; he was the Heaven-sent tonic that gladdened the company and kept us from sheer madness.

"My boys," he would say with a grin, dragging one leg from eighteen inches of slush, "there's mud *and* mud, but this is the most remarkable specimen I've ever struck." He got a tin, and grabbing a handful of the stuff slammed it inside and closed the lid. "That goes home as a memento," he explained.

Told in the Huts.

The spring came along and the mud vanished. Our hearts rose with the awakening of Nature, and life seemed not so terrible.

Then the strange thing happened. "Earwig" got a pass home, and came back after five days. But it was hardly "Earwig" that came back—it was someone different. No more the song and the jest, no more the light-hearted, careless man, but someone who came into the trench with a grim, set face and eyes that burned.

In vain we strove to find a reason for this great change, for he was uncommunicative, and merely smiled a wan smile when somebody timidly mentioned the subject. It was I who eventually succeeded in piecing together the true story, and I am glad I did so, for it enabled me to see the largeness of his heart.

"Earwig" lived in a London suburb not far from my own home, and while on leave I visited the place with the ostensible purpose of gaining information. It was, however, not from any motive of mere inquisitiveness, but because I wondered if it was financial trouble, or something from which the "boys" could help to extricate him. In a barber's shop I found out the truth, and knew how powerless we were to assist him.

It was his wife. She had sold up the home, taken her two children, and gone off with another man—and all the time "Earwig" was labouring and suffering "out there." I was sick at the knowledge of it, and tortured to think that we could do nothing in the world to help him; nothing to bring back his cheerful smile and the joyful spirit which was life to those who knew and loved him.

Back again to the trenches. But I said no word to the boys nor to "Earwig," but I watched him carefully and saw the depth of his mental agony. Little by little I spoke of home, and so dragged in incoherent instalments—a confirmation of the story from his own lips. But never a word

"Earwig."

of disparagement of the woman passed his lips. He could think no wrong of her—she had been his ideal, and he refused to have it shattered.

He never told me exactly what had happened, but I think he knew that I was in possession of his secret.

It was after the great attack that the end came. We had gone "over the top" early in the morning, and the fighting was bitter and long. I can remember seeing old "Earwig" with his head down and a glint in his grey eyes, and then all that followed is a blank, until we had taken over a length of the enemy's front trench and consolidated it.

Then I saw "Earwig" again. He was lying mortally wounded in a corner of the trench, waiting for the R.A.M.C. men. How he had managed to get there I don't know. He was dying fast, and before the Padre could come, he was gone. Just before the end he recovered consciousness, and somebody told me that he wanted me. I went over to him and took the hand that he tried to hold out.

"Chum," he whispered, "if ever you should see her—you know who I mean—just tell her not to—not to—worry. Of course, it was all a mistake. She never meant to hurt me. It must have been very lonely for her—over there. She didn't know what she was doing, old man. She was always like that, quick to act, and regretting it afterwards. . . . Tell her I love her just as I did that day—that day. Where are you, chum?—it's very dark. . . . Yes, just you tell her—I—I love her, and not to fear—God will put it right one day. Tell her I'll be waiting—then——"

The hand in mine grew cold, and I saw that the life had gone from him. And that was how he died, forgiving, noble-hearted to the end; refusing to believe ill of the woman he had made his idol. To me such a sin as she had committed seemed beyond all pardon, but perhaps he was right, and one day God would straighten things out.

The Bravery of Women.

THE following true narrative is but one splendid example among many of the bravery shown by Belgian women under conditions of exceptional danger. The incident occurred in a village not remote enough from the war zone to be free from the anxiety of raids by enemy aircraft.

In pre-war days that village was a typical scene of peaceful, homely life, where the peasants devoted their thrifty lives to pursuits that were as far removed from the horror of human slaughter as pole is set from pole. The white cottages nestled behind the twisted branches of wistaria and vine, and the poplars stood like sentinels along the straight, cobbled roads. There was a simple Calvary at the entrance to the churchyard, where the face of the Christ looked down upon all who passed that way, reminding them that the infinite understanding of finite sorrows was greater and more sublime than the human suffering of which He was the world's supreme example.

On one side of the church stood the humble cottage of the Curé, a saintly old man, who had done no harm—by thought or deed—during all the long years he had lived among his beloved flock. Upon the other side was a convent, known throughout the whole country-side for the sympathy and kindly help which was never denied when sought. It was also the local school where the young girls of the village attended for their limited education.

It was only when the terror-stricken fugitives of the villages further east began to hurry along the road beneath the poplar-trees, that they vaguely began to understand that ghastly pageant in the aftermath of war.

Armoured Cruiser.

The Bravery of Women.

Old men, mumbling broken words of horror at the scenes they had left behind them beyond that far horizon; women, white-faced and dumb with loathing and fear, but whose eyes were eloquent of the shame that is nameless; young children, clinging to the parent skirts, and sobbing because the whole world—as their little lives had known it—had suddenly changed, and they were frightened. Strange, incredible stories—tales of unspeakable things—began to be made known throughout the village, and the men and the women who heard them shook their heads as their eyes turned to the figure of the Christ at the roadside.

It was from the full sunshine of God's heaven that the first message of Death was sent. Bombs were dropped upon that little, white village as though it were the most important arsenal or munition factory in Europe. One explosive bomb fell upon the church with a blasphemous sound, as though all hell had been let loose—hungry and defiant. Another bomb fell close to the cottage of the Curé, making a cruel wound in his beloved garden.

An anxious, frightened crowd had assembled in the road outside the churchyard gate—fearful of even whispering their thoughts to one another. Their hushed words rose faint in the smoke of the blurred sunlight.

Then a wonderful thing happened—something far more wonderful than the scientific murder of innocent women and children. For the great iron gates of the convent garden opened, and a silent procession of women and children moved slowly towards where the village crowd was waiting. First of all came the Reverend Mother, with her face lifted to the blue sky above her, and her lips moving in silent prayer. Her thin, delicate hands were crossed upon her breast, and the sunlight touched the silver cross she wore. Behind her followed the young girls and little children—very quiet and orderly, but with questioning looks upon their pale faces. Last of all came the Sisters of the House. There was no

Told in the Huts.

suggestion of panic—no disorder—no lack of discipline, though the war fiend had come to within a hundred yards of their sacred home.

Slowly the procession moved towards the Calvary, and instinctively every man and woman present knelt in prayer. With her arms raised towards the carved figure in front of her, and in a voice that could be heard, clear and confident, above the sobs of her listeners, the Reverend Mother called aloud her prayer to heaven.

But the words she uttered were not those of supplication for protection from the horrors that were closing in so near to themselves. She left that to the great Protector of all. They were words of womanly solicitude for the brave men who were suffering the agonies of death and degradation upon the battle-field—for the women who were forced to endure what was even worse than the bloodiest wounds of warfare. It was for the safety and the honour of her country that she invoked the Divine aid. Her own danger, and that of the dear ones around her, were forgotten.

Her prayer was a very short one, and so simple in language that the meaning of each word went straight to every heart. When she had finished, she paused in silence, and the comfort that her words had given now shone from eyes that had been dull with terror and dim with tears.

With a queenly dignity she moved from the spot where she had stood, and the little procession reformed in the same order as that in which it had come. Without even deigning to look at the devilish havoc that had been caused around her, she led her children back to the hitherto unbroken sanctuary of the convent walls, and with her own frail hands she closed the iron gates.

Slowly, and with hushed whispers, the villagers dispersed, and the road became deserted once more. The only figure left there was that of the Christ upon the Cross—and the shadow it cast was set towards the ruined church behind it.

French

"Cook's Mate."

By Gunner L. T., R.G.A.

Our Chef

To-day has been my day of days. That is to say I have officiated in the capacity of "Cook's Mate." This select method of killing time may probably be as far from your ken as the laws of Rameses, or the strange rites of the Babylonians.

To begin with, you confront the chief cook's man, robed in his garb of office—a filthy scowl and a pair of what to my vision (see medical form) appeared to be white ducks. Under the scrutiny of his Prometheus-like glance one is naturally expected to wither. That I failed to do so, apparently sent me up several degrees in his estimation, for he bestowed upon me a perfectly melting smile—and we commenced work. I took my stand in front of a mountain of bread, cruelly vivisected into Brobdingnagian slices, and waited. I should mention that, an hour before opening time, three hungry soldiers were waiting on the doorstep with basin and plate, flourishing their knives and forks alarmingly. My chief cook's man, who had probably been a "bruiser" in his early and lamented youth, told them off with an enviable display of choice vernacular, and slammed the door in their faces.

"Glory be, the shpalpins!" he muttered. "They waits every morning from sevin till eight, and meself workin' me guts out to git the rations and all!"

Shortly after he opened the door, and a string of men commenced an assault upon the "mates." Like lightning I slammed three pieces of bread into each man's plate, and my near neighbour hurled one pint of tea into each basin,

Told in the Huts.

while another fiercely bayoneted a rasher of bacon and supplemented the dose. The tomatoes which followed added tone to the concoction, and the partly pacified string of men distributed themselves around the tables and endeavoured to get outside it all.

Now you might imagine that this job was the acme of simplicity, but, alas! it has its drawbacks. For instance, there are the crusty pieces of bread to be disposed of, and to do this in any peaceable manner one ought to have every man's medical sheet to refer to, for the men with bad teeth absolutely refuse to touch it. When I tried to "palm off" several pieces upon an innocent-looking lamb, he assured me with tears in his eyes that he was under dental treatment. Next man ditto, next ditto, until I came to the dreadful conclusion that the Company is composed of toothless men—alas!

The man with the tea had an equally thankless task. He was supposed to give a round pint and no more. When he precipitated the deluge into the capacious basin the recipient would still stand stark still with a pathetic look, and an eloquent expression in his eyes, but the tea-man was adamant and the very flower of inscrutability. Nothing could move him. It invariably ended in a staring competition in which my man always won, but it didn't seem quite fair, because he always retained the advantage in the shape of the pint measure.

There were all kinds of subterfuge to be overcome, for men in khaki are as like as two peas, and when a man chose to depart from the ways of virtue and to finish his breakfast, wash up his plate and basin, and insinuate himself for the second time into the waiting queue, it needed a Sherlock Holmes to detect him. I spotted one man who had been careless enough to leave a few drops of tea in the bottom of his basin, but he practised his deception so well that it seemed worth the additional pint.

"Cook's Mate."

Half-an-hour later, when all the "prog" had miraculously disappeared, we set to work to gather up the fragments that remained. This feat was carried out by means of gymnastic gyrations. Two men mounted the tables and hustled the crumbs, bits of bacon-rind, and tomato-skins, plus sundry adhesive substances, into two baths, which the remaining cook's man held at one end of the tables. These tables are mounted on trestles, and the noise created by twelve stone of human tissue rushing about all over them is appalling—luckily we were all clad in the canvas shoes which are supplied for use on the gun platforms. This done, we learned to our horror that the office of cook's mate involved the washing of the tables and floor. The tables proved an easy task, but the floor was a sisyphean labour. Before I had time to vent my spite on the huge "scrubber" which someone shoved in my hand, I recoiled before a three-inch wall of water which seethed from the opposite doorway, behind which hovered two grinning men with a huge empty bath, watching with apparent glee their handiwork. It seemed that additional labour had been imported for this operation, for on every side some grey-shirted acrobat was pushing a scrubber, a squeegee, a mop, or any implement which would defend him from the flood, and every man's sole ambition seemed to be to push the now turbulent stream of mud over my shoe-tops. I don't know who won, but I have an idea some of them will be busy to-night if they hope to be fit for Church Parade to-morrow. Afterwards we scrubbed down the asphalt outside the "dining-hall," and Noah's flood paled into insignificance before the deluge of water employed in this task—I never thought there was so much water in all the world. Dreadnoughts could have floated in it. The Battle of Jutland could have been re-fought outside that Hut. I think the other chaps got a bit of their own back there, but I didn't care, I had had my day.

At dinner-time the process was repeated, but before tea

Preparing Dinner

Told in the Huts.

I convinced the chief cook's man, by eloquent peroration, that urgent family matters rendered my services imperative elsewhere, and I " clicked," as they say here.

I have been reckoning up the casualties—one pair trousers, one pair socks, a shirt, one pair canvas shoes (not fatal), a certain loss of dignity and virtue, and an overwhelming sense of defeat in the latter half of the combat. One ought really to carry a 9.2 and armour plating for these orgies. Next time I shall be better prepared.

Barrack Square Ovens

On the Way Back.

By A. St. John Adcock.

They emerged from the booking-office as if they had been hurrying, and the elder woman looked round for the station clock.

"Oh, plenty of time," she said; "another eight minutes yet."

The girl who was with her made no response. You guessed they were mother and daughter. The mother was a hearty woman, nearing sixty, with a ruddy, good-natured, strong-featured face, and a managing, reliable manner. She was not poorly dressed, but serviceably, as one dresses who has to count her money more than once before she spends it. Her hands were roughened with work; she wore a sensible plaid shawl, for there was snow on the railway lines and on the fields beyond, and capping all the houses round about. The daughter was a slight girl of some seventeen years, pale, anxious, pre-occupied, seeming rather as if she were hurt and suffering, and shrank from being noticed.

"Look here, now, Annie," said the mother, speaking firmly and swiftly, "if you can't leave off crying, run back home at once, like a good girl. Don't upset him. I want him to go feeling cheerful and comfortable about us."

"I'm not crying," the girl protested feebly.

"You are. You know you are. And I won't have him upset. Don't be unkind to him—just you run off at once. He'll be here in a minute."

Told in the Huts.

"But—but he'll think it so funny——" The girl struggled with her words.

"No, he won't. I'll explain. I'll make it right. It's much kinder to him. And you've said good-bye once, when I was hoping you wouldn't come. Run home, now, there's a dear, and leave it to me."

She put a hand on the girl's arm to urge her towards the door, and, after a momentary hesitation, she moved with quickening steps and disappeared into the booking-office. She was running her hardest over the level crossing a hundred yards further up the line, as a bronzed young soldier in khaki came from the booking-office and joined the old lady on the platform.

"Well," she greeted him breezily, "everything all right? Got your ticket?"

"Yes; that's all right." He was buttoning something into a breast pocket that was over-full. A tall, personable fellow, he carried a rifle, had a prodigious kit-bag strapped on his back, and a water-bottle and divers tightly packed small parcels hanging from his waist-belt. "They'd take me for Santa Claus, only it isn't Christmas," he grinned, surveying his burdens; then, abruptly, "Where's Annie?"

"Oh, she's all right," said the mother, easily. "I had to send her back. Silly thing! We forgot and left the gas-ring alight, and I don't want the house burnt down. Hope we haven't forgot anything else." She fingered the tight parcels critically. "Be sure you put these oil-skin socks on over your other ones when you go into them damp trenches. And mind you wear the thick new vest." She shook a warning finger at him. "You want me out there to look after you, you're so terrible careless!"

They both laughed.

"Annie and me are hard at it knitting you some more, and if you don't wear them I shall be very angry with you."

"I'll wear 'em, you bet," he said, "but don't make

On the Way Back.

too many of 'em. You've got enough to do. Wish I could get you a bigger allowance—I don't like you taking in that blessed washing."

"Nonsense! I'm glad to be doing something."

"If you can't let the rooms," he went on, "I'd sooner you sold some of the things and went into some lodgings."

"I shan't do nothing of the sort," she insisted. "I'm going to have the home waiting there ready for you when you come back. Don't you fear; I'll manage."

He grumbled vaguely.

"Now, I tell you, you're not to fidget about me and Annie," she reproved him. "We're as right as could be, and there's no need. I'm not worriting. Your father went all through the Boer War and came back safe, didn't he? Very well, then, and so will you. I only wish he was still alive—he'd be out there with you, I know that! I sometimes get a feeling how angry he must be now because he can't go."

"Ah, he was a good pluck'd one, he was," said the soldier.

"When I get your medals to hang alongside his, I shall be as proud as a dog with two tails."

They both laughed again, but his laugh was not so cheery as hers. He was restless, uneasy, as if the strain of parting was telling on him; but she was as unconcerned and as practical as if he had been merely going up to an office in town and would be home again, as usual, in the evening. When the gates of the level-crossing swung open, and they could hear the train approaching, one felt there was even a touch of relief in his, "Here it comes!" but she only said briskly, with no change of tone:

"Mind you send me a post card directly you get out there, and write when you can."

"That's all right," he said.

Then, as the train fussed noisily in, they kissed each

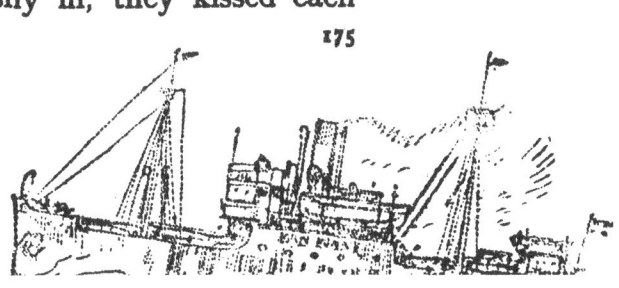

Told in the Huts.

other, and she put her hands on his broad shoulders to pull him down and kiss him a second time, just in a good, motherly fashion, and without a flicker of emotion on her comfortable face.

"Annie'll be too late," he observed, leaning from the carriage window.

"Yes, silly thing. Never mind. She said good-bye once. I'll say it again for you, and she can write."

He took off his cap and waved it as the train carried him off, and hung out, waving it as long as he was within sight.

"Good-bye," she shouted, and "Good luck!" and stood sturdily in the middle of the platform gazing after him. She did not take out a handkerchief; she waved, and kept waving, one of her rough hands; but when the train had gone so far that she could have been no more than an outline to the other's eyes, her lips were quivering and tears streaming unheeded down her cheeks, and I turned away.

Trenching under Fire

"Little Toots."

WE were all in the best of spirits that morning—at least those of us who were left—for we had captured a German trench during the night, and our blood had not yet had time to cool. There was not a man among us who would not have jumped at any chance of taking on a job that meant risk or danger, and the more dangerous the risk was, the better he would have liked it. So there were plenty of volunteers who offered to go out and mend the telephone wire which had gone wrong during our skirmish of the night.

It was as good as asking for certain death, for it meant crossing the open ground in full daylight, and within easy reach of the enemy bullets, to a spot about fifty yards distant.

We all of us rather wondered that "Little Toots" was chosen for the honour. My own opinion was, and still is, that he did not know a telephone from an empty sardine tin. However, the smaller a man is, the less there is to hit, and there was not much of him at the best of times, when food was cheap and plentiful. He was little more than an apology of a man after a few months in the trenches, and the only thing he was really clever at was whistling tunes between his wizen little hands. He was top-hole at that. That was why we called him "Toots." His real name was Horace.

He was as proud as Punch when he found that he was the lucky man, and he looked a good couple of inches longer in his body as he crawled over the sand-bags. We all wished him the best of luck, for he was a popular little fellow among the boys, and he had cheered many a dug-out with his music.

Told in the Huts.

He reached the spot all right, though how he dodged the bullets was a marvel. We watched him cautiously, and saw him stoop to pick up the wire. Then the good fortune, which had taken him there in safety, deserted him. He was shot in the arm and leg almost at the same instant. He fell to the ground as helpless and as useless as the telephone he had gone to mend.

But the job had to be finished, and now there was "Toots" to be rescued before any more mischief was done. My pal Jim was the next man chosen.

Now Jim stood over six foot in his stockings, and had a head of red hair which was a danger signal for miles around, so it was not likely that he would escape the same fate that had come to "Toots." I never did believe in miracles myself, but if ever I saw one performed it was then. Like many big men, Jim was not given to indulging in any excess of energy, and, to put it mildly, he was one of those fellows who were born a bit tired. Do you think he was going to hurry himself upon this occasion? Not a bit of it. I will not repeat what he said about the German who had bowled over "Little Toots," but he did not pay him any compliments. He just got out of the trench as though he was stepping out of a nice, warm bath, and off he went straight to where Toots was writhing upon the ground.

It was then that the miracle happened, for, in spite of him being in full view of both trenches, and with the bullets hissing round him, he did not get so much as a scratch. He had been an engineer's mechanic before he joined up, and what he did not know about a telephone was not worth learning. That is why we saw him fix up the machine in about as long a time as it took poor "Toots" to look at it. Having done so, he stooped quickly, and lifted the wounded man in his great arms, and carried him in such a way that his own body was a shelter from the firing-line.

Back he came, and you bet there was no loafing about

"Little Toots."

the business this time. He had not cared a jot about danger to his own great carcase when he was alone, but now he had a wounded pal to save. As he dropped the unconscious "Toots" into my arms, he turned and shook his big fist at the German trenches. Then he shouted out at the top of his voice :

"This ain't my wedding, you blighters, so ye need not have wasted so much of yer blooming confetti."

"Little Toots" is now in England, with both his arm and leg in slings, and I think the happiest moment in his life was when he heard that Jim had received the D.C.M. as a reward for his pluck upon the occasion stated above.

A Lewis Gun in Action

Drawn by Private MacMichael, Middlesex Regt.

SOUVENIR HUNTERS.

The "Night Hawks."

By Levorno Sabatini.

There was no fluster, no bustle—we had passed beyond that stage—as the mechanics tuned up the 'planes, and the pilots, with an expert touch here and there, tested and made ready for the day's orders. The aerodrome was one of the largest in France, with huge sheds and canvas shelters, daubed with many-coloured fantastic designs, which faded into the atmosphere and shadows, making their detection from a distance a difficult matter for the enemy observers. The flying-men, sauntering around, coolly smoking cigarettes, had been specially chosen for their proved courage, initiative, and intrepidity. They were placed conveniently to the fighting lines, and their special work was to check enemy observation, and give battle in the air, and most of the squadron had a good string of enemy machines to their credit.

There was Melton, a well-set-up fellow from Hudson Bay, a boy of twenty-two or twenty-three in years, but a man in experience of aerial fighting. His special chum was Jeffries, from Alberta, at the foot of the Rockies. Both had lived a strenuous life in the open, full of adventure, but had left it to assist the cause of the old Motherland, and had been brought together during their course of training. It was rumoured that the Herr Commandant had set a price upon the heads of Melton and Jeffries, but little they cared for that. Their machines were called "Night Hawk Major" and "Night Hawk Minor," so nicknamed by the rest of the squadron owing to their many daring flights at night, and the names had stuck.

Told in the Huts.

As they waited, an orderly approached Melton with a message, saying that he and Jeffries were wanted at Headquarters. Wondering what new adventure they were about to embark upon, they presented themselves to the O.C., who, without preamble, asked if they had any suggestion to make which might lead to the discovery and destruction of a nest of enemy hornets, which had been causing trouble, and which we had been unable to locate.

Melton turned to Jeff, and said in his slow, drawling way:

"Well, I think we might evolve something. Eh, Jeff?"

"Take your time, then, boys, and think it over, and remember that everything you require is at your disposal, but the sooner the job is done the better, for the officers of the 18th —— have been twitting me on those rascals beating us at our own game."

Melton and Jeffries went outside, quiet and thoughtful.

"So the Old Man has had his leg pulled," said Melton.

"'Pears so," replied Jeff. "It's up to us to scotch these beggars. Got a proposition?"

Melton was thinking hard, and for a few minutes did not reply. Then he murmured, half to himself,

"Might be done that way, p'r'aps."

"Which way?" asked Jeff.

"Well," said Melton, "this ain't a job for a crowd, it's for you and I, and the 'Herr Bird' to show us where he lives."

"Say, Melton, think he will ask us to tea?"

"No, but we will track him home. You have noticed that all the enemy machines of that squad are of a new type and easily distinguishable. For the past week every evening at dusk one of these fellows has visited our lines for a last look round. I have observed that he always arrives from a certain direction, a roundabout way, but always takes a straight course on his return. Now this fellow is not fond

The "Night Hawks."

of flying in the dark—none of them are—from which I logically conclude that when he has seen enough he makes a bee-line for home before lighting-up time. What we have to do is this. When he comes to-night, we must make him stay longer than he intended by getting Weston to cut off his retreat. If Weston can hold him for an hour it will be dark, and then we take up the game and run him to earth."

"How can we do that in the dark?" asked Jeffries.

"Way out yonder," said Melton, jerking his thumb in the direction of a locality twelve thousand miles away, "we used to track a particularly destructive beast—not unlike those in manners we are after now—which lay doggo all day, only coming out at night to drink and feed. His first performance when he reached the pool was to drink his fill, and then roll and wallow on the bank. That was his undoing. We used to spread a luminous preparation on the banks in the day-time which absorbed light, and at night-time our friend used to pick it up on his thick dark hide, and we could detect him—or at least the luminous patches—a good distance away, as he prowled through the forest, and pick him off with ease. What we have to do now is to drop some of this stuff on the wings of the enemy 'plane and follow him home without ourselves being discovered. This we should be able to do, as his noisy engine will prevent him hearing us, and given a dark night, and flying at a high altitude, he will also be unable to see us."

"Good," said Jeff; "it's as nice a wild-goose chase as any I ever heard of, but I can think of nothing better. We have some hours to spare; you go over to the Engineers and prepare your paint, and I will find up Weston and tell him exactly what we require him to do. He had better use the big 'plane, it's a bit faster. Meet me here at five o'clock; it will be quite dark by seven."

Melton went over to the Engineers' Camp, and with their help prepared a good supply of luminous paint, leaving it to

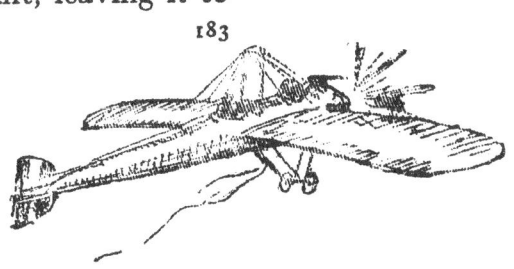

Told in the Huts.

absorb the strong sunlight in a large open vessel. Murphy asked him if he was " going to paint a rainbow or alter the sky-line," but received little satisfaction by way of reply. Jeff sought out Weston, and explained the scheme so far as his part went. He was to go up on the big 'plane directly he saw the enemy approaching, and manœuvre to hold him over our lines until darkness set in, but on no account was he to bring him down. Three flashes at intervals was to be the signal for his descent.

At five o'clock Melton and Jeffries met and arranged for the luminous liquid, together with a projector fitted with a long flexible tube to be fixed on " Night Hawk Major," one of the powerful fliers recently sent over by the R.A.F., then wheeled their machine to a suitable position for ascent, screened by a belt of trees, ready to take up the chase.

The sky was overcast with low hanging clouds, giving promise of a very dark night, while the wind was blowing in the desired direction—towards the Camp. About six o'clock the light was fading, and a sharp look-out was kept for our aerial visitor. Sure enough he was soon spotted coming from his usual direction and flying high. We knew, however, that he would descend considerably for observation purposes, and Weston, whose engine was running, ascended as the Hun passed over our heads and turned to make his return journey. Then commenced one of the most thrilling exhibitions of flying tactics ever seen. We watched with bated breath, silent and tense. Weston was using a powerful and very fast battle-plane, mounted with a machine-gun; his adversary using a smaller machine of a new type, very speedy and easy to handle, but carrying no gun. On he came, the while Weston was ascending in a dizzy spiral to gain the upper position. The enemy, thinking he was about to be attacked by a heavier machine, put on all speed to make for home, wasting no time in climbing. It looked, too, as if he would make his escape, when down came Weston

The "Night Hawks."

like a hawk pouncing on its prey, descending slantingly at a tremendous pace, straight for the Hun, until it looked as if the two machines must converge and collide in mid-air. Fritz saw what must happen in time, and quickly veered round and banked to avoid the crash. It was a clever movement, but it brought him over our lines again, which was exactly Weston's object. Then the two began to rise again, up, up in ever narrowing circles, straight up, until in the gathering twilight the eye could hardly follow them. Like a bolt from the heavens the German suddenly planed down right under Weston's machine in the direction of home, and it looked a thousand to one chance that this time he would get away. We groaned aloud in our anxiety. Weston was obliged to complete his circle before facing in the right direction, then off he went like an arrow, crowding on all speed the engines were capable of. Here was a test indeed. Could our home-built engine beat the best the enemy had produced? We had no doubt about the *man;* would the machine back him up and enable him to make good? Anxiously we watched the two, now only faintly discernible in the distant sky. The sport of the thing entered our soul, and worked us up to an intense pitch of excitement. The two machines certainly seemed to be drawing nearer to each other, whether it was actually so, or only a trick of perspective we could not be sure. Then the direction seemed to change; they appeared to be bending round, like the horses at the far end of the race-course. Yes! Weston was heading him off, pressing him more and more on the right, forcing the enemy to wind to the left, until at last he was facing our lines again—the Hun in front, Weston behind—driving him. Then we knew our engine had made good, and we were again on top. On they came, Fritz first turning to one side, then the other, Weston following every turn with a similar one. It was a nerve-shattering experience for the Hun, for he must have realised that Weston was playing with him as a cat plays

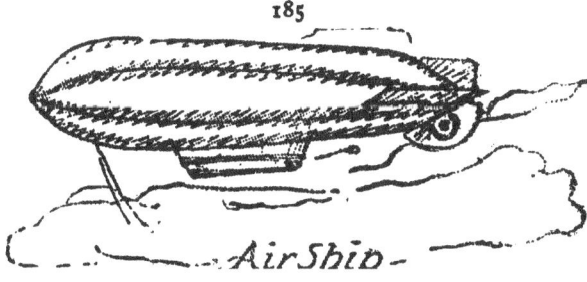

Told in the Huts.

with a mouse, that he could be sent crashing to his death at the will of his opponent. Purple shadows were gathering on the hills and under the trees, and darkness was silently clothing the earth in its mantle, when Weston's signal to descend was made. So well had he done his work that at seven o'clock the two machines were practically in the same place over our lines as when the contest started.

We knew that Melton and Jeffries were up and ahead somewhere, though out of sight, and when Weston safely alighted in that dangerous light we gave him a rousing cheer to relieve our pent-up feelings, while his late opponent darted off like a swallow going home in autumn—not understanding, but thankful for his escape.

Melton and Jeffries were flying at a great altitude when Fritz passed underneath them. They allowed him to fly slightly ahead, then gradually planed down until both were flying at nearly the same level, Fritz, perhaps, being a hundred yards or so lower. Both were flying at an immense pace, but by coaxing the engine, as Melton well knew how, he gradually overhauled his enemy, hand over hand, until he appeared to be flying exactly above him. Jeffries was ready to let fly the luminous paint at a word from Melton, and was getting anxious, for he knew he would lose sight of his object as the night became darker.

"Try a little," said Melton, above the drone of the engine; and out shot from the end of the tube, a few yards below, a column of the liquid, gleaming faintly phosphorescent as it fell, but just short of its object.

"Speed up a bit," said Jeffries.

"'Fraid she won't do another yard, but I'll try, replied Melton. Then after a pause, "Drop some more, Jeff!"

This time it fell too much to the right, and Melton said, "I'll dip slightly. Watch your chance."

A little ground was lost in making this manœuvre, but again made up in a few minutes, and Jeff, watching

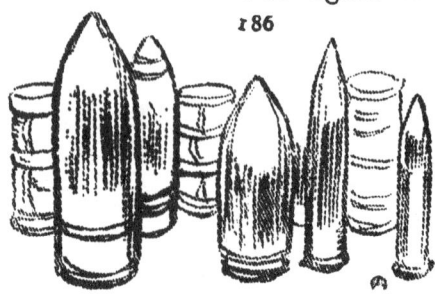

The " Night Hawks."

intently, for it was now difficult to discern anything, judged that he was right over his object, and shot out a good supply of his preparation. To his delight it seemed to stop in mid-air, and he knew that it had fallen and spread over the wings of the enemy's 'plane.

Their first object achieved, Melton gradually ascended and dropped behind, keeping his eyes fixed on that luminous patch ahead, and leading his opponent to believe that he had at last shaken off his pursuers. The airmen were convinced that Fritz would now fly straight home, for, they reasoned, he would be too much shaken up by his long encounter with Weston to think of anything else, while there would be no other aerodrome prepared to assist his descent. On they flew through the black night; no object could be seen, save that luminous trail in front, glowing in the darkness. Hours seemed to have passed, since they took up the chase, before there dimly appeared far ahead a circle of small twinkling lights, which gradually became larger and clearer as they approached.

"We are nearly there," whispered Melton. "Yonder is the Hun's aerodrome, and they are waiting up for him."

Descending to a lower altitude they searched around for landmarks to determine their whereabouts, when far below them, like a ribbon winding this way and that, reflecting the flames on the higher grounds, they dimly discerned what they knew to be a river. Anxiously they scanned it, trying to recognise its twistings and bridges, calculated the mileage they had made and direction, until they felt sure they would be able to locate their object again in daylight.

"The end of the trail," said Melton. "Now for home."

* * * * * *

Next morning Melton and Jeffries again presented themselves at Headquarters.

Told in the Huts.

" Glad to see you back, boys," said the O.C. ; " what luck did you have ? "

The two airmen reported their adventures briefly, and asked for the large scale map. Studying this carefully for a few minutes, Melton put his pencil on a certain spot, saying :

" There is your nest of hornets, in the bend of that river."

The officer congratulated them on their initiative and courage, and reaching for a book, made certain recommendations opposite their names.

" You will pilot the squadron to-morrow morning and exterminate them," he said.

* * * * * *

Official Report :
" An aviation squadron dropped bombs on the German aerodrome at Mannheim on the Rhine early yesterday morning, and entirely destroyed sheds and aeroplanes. All our aviators returned safely."

" How did you locate him ? " asked Weston on their return.

" Dropped salt on his tail," laconically replied Jeffries.

Battle Plane

The Gasper.

THE UNOFFICIAL ORGAN of the 18th, 19th, 20th and 21st (P.S.) ROYAL FUSILIERS.

No. 12.   JANUARY 29, 1916.   PRICE { England, One Penny. France, 10c.—Deux Sous

JOCK ON LEAVE IN LONDON.
"Hoots! but it's a Gerrman flare, I'd be welcomin' the noo."

NOTICE.—We expect to publish soon, if accurate particulars can be obtained, a Special Supplement, being the Casualty Lists for the four U.P.S. Battalions.

All contributions to be sent to Private G. M. Green, No. 409, D Company, 19th Royal Fusiliers, B.E.F.

Copies of the ordinary issues may be obtained for 1½d., post free to any address in the United Kingdom, or 2d. to the B.E.F., from the Publishers, Messrs. Bennett Brothers, *Journal* Office, Salisbury; also from Mr. A. E. Pool, Newsagent, 55, George Street, Oxford. If a larger sum is sent, copies will be sent weekly till the subscription is exhausted, and in the event of *The Gasper* coming to an untimely end, the balance will be returned. Men who have been in the habit of sending copies home or to friends, please note.

All rights of reproduction of cartoons reserved by the Proprietors. Applications should be addressed to the Publishers.

A reproduction of one of the numerous Trench Magazines which have come into existence as a result of the War, and which typify the spirit of our soldiers in the field. The present example is reproduced by kind permission of the Editor and Messrs. Bennett Brothers, Salisbury.

Metamorphosis.

"A prophet hath no honour in his own country." So runs the proverb, or text or quotation, or whatever it may be, and the truth of the assertion is proven every day. But that an *Englishman* has no honour, or rather no appreciation, in his own country is, if possible, even more true. He is a modest individual, given to introspection and painfully aware of his own shortcomings, and this trait in his character has drawbacks, although to "know thyself" would seem to be the first step towards real wisdom.

We as a nation are wont to depreciate ourselves too greatly.

We are wiser than we are aware of, and the prestige of Englishmen abroad shows that other nations value our capabilities more highly than we do ourselves. The Scotsman has not this English trait; he appraises himself more truly, and as a man, previous to intimate acquaintanceship, must necessarily be taken at his own valuation, the Southerner suffers.

It is only required to take the case of the U.P.S. in order to prove the truth of this contention. We laughed at our training, derided the seemingly illogical and ill-ordered pathway which was supposed to lead us towards efficiency, but we laughed too soon. Whether by accident or design, methinks we now realise that our training has been logical and thorough, the gradual process of preparation through which we have passed being the most perfect that could be conceived for fitting the civilian to meet the tremendous test of active service.

We started in cosy, comfortable billets, *sans* rifles, *sans* equipment, *sans* packs, in fact *sans* everything uncomfortable. We acquired rifles temporarily and then permanently; we made route marches in civilian clothes without any of the trappings of war, and gradually added to our burdens until something approaching "full marching order" was attained. From billets we moved into camp, an ideal camp which in retrospect we have learned to love. Another move took us North and introduced less ideal conditions. Our last trek Southward may have been for better or for worse, according to the point of view, but at any rate it taught us to rely on our own resources for amusement and cut us off from the allurements of a town; also there were bivouacs!

Our move overseas put us under snow-covered canvas, and our railway travelling was well-calculated to inure us to discomfort, and then at last we came to the trenches! But we were ready for them; we walked into them with the sangfroid of an experienced lion-tamer entering a den of wild animals. There was no nervousness, no shock to our civilian sensibilities, for these had been deadened by the hardening process to which they had been subjected. We were used even to fire conditions, for marking on the ranges at B—— was excellent preparation. And thus we have become soldiers, gradually and thoroughly, in short wonderfully, for it is absolutely inconceivable that we could have taken our places in the line so worthily without this steady, well-ordered, comparative training course.

The same process still continues even out here. Without intending a grumble, it is not untrue to say we go from bad to worse, and each step we take is in preparation for the one that follows. We have experienced cold weather, wet weather, mud in abundance, snipers, rifle grenades, machine-gun fire, trench mortar fire, German mines, and bombardment, so we can feel ready for almost anything.

The beauty of the system is that we can look back on all previous experiences with something like pleasure in the light of the next step. How cosy a draughty barn under shell fire feels after a sojourn in dug-out-less trenches; what a haven of rest the trenches appear when one goes out on working patrol at night and is spotted by the Bosches; and what a cushy job a night patrol will seem when we go over the parapet in broad daylight!

Yes, there is more method in our muddling than we are wont to admit, for it is something very like a miracle that can cause a clerkly civilian to regard a shell-shattered barn as a palace, a dish of hot Army stew a banquet fit for the gods, a few hours' undisturbed rest a dream of Elysium, and a letter from dear old Blighty a breath from Paradise.

STROZZI.

A Native of Northern France.

There is no more fascinating study than that of human nature. An interest in peoples and races (not Epsom) will provide a man with an ever-abiding hobby, absorbing, economical, and instructive. I am not a greatly travelled man, and a trip to France offered an opportunity to indulge my propensities for weighing and probing personalities, that appealed to me very strongly. We landed, and our hither and thither journey zigzagged seemingly all over France, but the particular specimen, genus, group or whatever science may dub it, never seemed to come my way. The native of Northern France, the product of this epoch-marking, earth-shaking hemisphere-hurling war seemed to elude me at every turn.

I seek it here, I seek it there,
In fact I seek it everywhere,
Is it in Heaven, or is it in Hell,
That damned elusive ——

Native of Northern France? I chanted dolefully, lamenting in the lyrical lines of the popular novel and play.

I began to despair, but my hopelessness was greeted with laughter.

"Natives? Don't you worry, you'll come across them right enough, and you won't be able to get rid of them."

For three weeks I sought assiduously, but in vain. Every moment was filled until it was only just occasionally that I could indulge in the luxury of a wash, while a bath was a dream of Elysium, a mirage that ever receded. When at the lowest ebb of expectancy I suddenly came in contact with the object of my quest, and I shall never forget the sensation with which I realised that my search was ended, my goal reached.

'Twas in a barn and far into the night that we first met.

We had arrived late, tired and footsore, and ready to sleep on the thin edge of a knife if necessary. A layer of straw covered the barn floor, and a more enticing bed never yet seduced my senses. I threw my length into what in reality was a grey and grimy couch, with the abandon of the bather who seeks relief from the scorching sun in the cool, crystal waters of a beautiful bathing pool.

I awoke with the sensation of having been awakened, and gradually I realised that my visitor, self-effacing, yet persistent, was the native of Northern France, so notorious, yet evasive; so populous, yet unpopular.

There is a kink in my nature which draws me towards the unpopular as a rule. There is usually a larger layer of personality on the well-hated creature than upon the popular favourite, and, therefore, I decided to study this specimen thoroughly and exhaustively. I began at once. Sleep left me, and although I tired in my efforts, I got no further rest until dawn, by which time I had learned not a little of the habits and idiosyncrasies of my long-sought subject.

There is a limit to man's patience, and after three weeks, during which we ate, drank, walked, and slept together, I began to tire of a companionship that had become irksome and even exceedingly distasteful to me. In vain I sought to rid myself of a faithful follower who had become an encumbrance. Possibly I had shown too much consideration in my first attention to the intruder, but he had certainly taken advantage of my good nature. I shortly found that not only was I his own strength and stay, but I was supporting a whole family—a progeny that was growing at an alarming rate. Their affection and attention were persistent—so much so that my health broke down beneath the strain, and I found myself one morning mouching mournfully along to Sick Parade. I came away with a glad eye, for the doctor got to the root of the trouble at once. "To get rid of them?" he queried. "one tin of Keatings and a bath!"

STROZZI.

Ruins.

If in the dawn of some serener day
Here from these ruins Life shall find new birth
And make to smile again this death-bound earth,
Hushing the callous clamour of the fray;
Then when the sun has pierced with vital ray
The darkness of drear desolation's dearth
These bleeding stones inheriting their worth
Shall guide the feet of Justice on their way.

O stones of sadness, standing silent there
The memory of what has been and shall be,
The witness to what ne'er shall be again.
By every blood-stain calling forth a prayer
There comes the day when those who cursed
shall flee.
There comes the hour that sanctifies your pain!

BOW WOW

DEFICIENCIES. I.

Private Jones—one rickshaw

W.H.WHEATCROFT.
12/Jan/16.

A Scrap of Paper.

A Burlesque in Three Acts and a Prologue, written by members of *The Gasper* staff, and presented at the "Grand Theatre," Billetville, on Christmas Eve, 1915.

[ALL RIGHTS RESERVED.]

DRAMATIS PERSONÆ.

CURLOCK COMBS	..	LIEUT. SKEY
	a super-detective.	
Dr. WATSON	..	SERGT. BASS
H.I.M. THE KAISER	..	LCE.-CPL. COTTAM
	a super-monarch.	
Lieut. MONTY MARLBOROUGH,		LIEUT. POWELL
	a super-swanker.	
S.M. FLETCHER	..	SERGT. HADLAND
	a super-sergeant.	
GABY	.. ..	PTE. FRANCIS
Mrs. Monty Marlborough, a super-sweetmeat.		
PROLOGUE	.. ..	PTE. SLARKE

PROLOGUE.

There is a tide in the affairs of men
Which, once omitted, never comes again.
We could not, for example, have a play
In leaky dugouts out Tra-la-la way;
So, when presented with so fair a palace,
To play no play would be most base and callous—
A Palace true—though Alfred Butt may sneer
But me no Butts! . . . they're Bulford way, not here!
And Alfred's Star, the beautiful Deslys—
Well, soon you'll see her daughter . . or her niece!
In fact the Stars (and all are stars you'll see)
May without treason rival Beerbohm Tree!
Such trivial defects as may mar the glory
Of this sublime and hair-uplifting story,
Uncertainty of action or of word
You'll pardon, Sirs. Give nobody the Bird . .
At least until to-morrow, when a turkey
Will be a gift to make them pleased and perky.
Rather than wonder if the merit's small,
The wonder is, there's any play at all!
For three short days, from Tuesday till to-day,
Sufficed to write and to rehearse the play;
And those three days we spent, as duty bade,
Chiefly upon fatigues and on parade—
Composed the words while rifles were inspected,
Confident that no dirt could be detected—
Practised the songs while standing in a queue
To draw gas-helmets or our dose of stew—
Rehearsed last night from six o'clock till eight,
And sought our final drinks, alas! too late.
You've *got* to laugh, for at this Season festive
Laughter's the only possible digestive;
And, to conclude, we wish you, free from sorrow,
A gorgeous gorge and sprightly spree to-morrow!

ACT I.

SCENE.—CURLOCK COMBS' DEN.

(*Table with breakfast laid, three chairs and couch, safe door in wall, Watson on couch R., reading newspaper.*) *Enter* CURLOCK *in his famous dressing gown.*

CURLOCK: Ah, Watson! Any news?
WATSON: Nothing interesting!
CURLOCK: My dear Watson, when will you learn wisdom! Never look for interest in a daily paper; look outside at the adverts.
WATSON (*nettled*): What can you get from advertisements? Listen to this for instance: "John Smith (late Kleinstein & Co.) has a choice assortment of breakfast sausages for sale. No German sausages for us—Rule Britannia!" Absurd, isn't it?
CURLOCK (*after deep thought*): You've hit it, Watson. I've been waiting for it for years, and now it's come!
WATSON (*mystified*): Well, it beats me. What—er—I suppose I may ask no questions?
CURLOCK (*irrelevantly*): My dear Watson, this den has seen more lions than Daniel ever dreamt of. First there was Joseph.
WATSON: Joseph? What Joseph? The man with the coat of many colours?
CURLOCK: No, the man with the house at many corners. You are more opaque than usual, Watson. Even your intelligence should be able to connect Joseph with Lyons.
WATSON: Great snakes! Of course.
CURLOCK: You yourself have seen potentates of every size, shape, colour, form, and smell standing here imploring my aid.
WATSON: Every King in Christendom and Heathendom I should say.
CURLOCK: Excepting one, Watson, excepting one. To-day is to see the vacancy filled.
WATSON: Why to-day?
CURLOCK: The paper, Watson! And if you wish for further confirmation lift the lid from the breakfast dish.
WATSON (*lifting dish cover*): German sausage!
CURLOCK (*smiling indulgently*): Are you convinced?
WATSON: I fail to follow you. I give it up.
CURLOCK: Heigho! You'll never make a corporal; I mean detective, Watson. To-day is to see the crowning pinnacle of my career. (*Poses dramatically.*) Listen, Watson! He comes!

(*A great noise is heard off—motor horns, explosions, and general clatter.*) *Enter* THE SUPREME WAR LORD *in Shining Armour.*

WATSON: Is this the man?
CURLOCK (*laconically*): Yep!
KAISER: Donner und blitzen! Donnervetter! Salmon and Gluckstein! Schweinhund!

Jones' long-expected parcel from Aunt Matilda turns out to contain a cardigan, some bed-socks, and a maconochie.

CURLOCK: He's asking you the name of your regiment! Now be careful, Watson.
KAISER: And which is Burlock der Grosser?
WATSON: He's come to the wrong shop. No compris! This isn't the grocer's.
KAISER: Burlock der Grosser, der great crime doctor!
CURLOCK: Curlock, Most High Mailyfist, spelt with a "C." Curlock Combs, detective, at your service.
KAISER: All great men spell their names with a K. K for Kaiser; K for Kultur. Henceforth you shall be Kurlock Kombs with a K.

(*Pins an Iron Cross on Curlock's chest.*)

CURLOCK: As you will, Hun of Huns. 'Tis useless to kick against a K, even in K boots at 3s. 4d.
KAISER: You are in my power, so I command your service. Might is right, even here, Herr Kurlock.
CURLOCK: As you say, I am in your power.
KAISER: I have a —
CURLOCK: You have a fleet of Zeppelins overhead, Most Flightiest.
KAISER: You are a klever man! How know you that?
CURLOCK: Elementary, my dear Kaiser, elementary. Association of ideas and sense of smell.
KAISER: Explain!
CURLOCK (*lifting cover of breakfast dish as though conjuring*): Here, German sausage! Smell—paraffin. Result Zeppelins! Nothing easier.
KAISER: Ach! Goot! You shall find the missing paper—or you shall be dropped from a Zeppelin from five miles high!
CURLOCK: Some drop, Watson. Ah, you want the dispatch, the paper?
KAISER: Then you know?
CURLOCK: Je sais tout! (*Takes up paper and reads.*) A dispatch of the utmost importance to the result of the war has been lost by an officer of the 19th Battalion Royal Fusiliers. The dispatch should have been addressed to Director Hector, and a fabulous reward has been offered for its recovery.—*Northcliffe News.*
KAISER (*pinning another Iron Cross on him*): You shall join my Secret Service.
CURLOCK: What do you think of that, Watson?
WATSON: I'll tell you later, Combs.
KAISER: Who is your silent friend?
CURLOCK: My friend, Most Supreme Sausage King, is the famous Dr. Watson.
KAISER: Watson! Watson! What does he do?
CURLOCK (*puzzled*): What *do* you do, Watson?
WATSON: Don't ask me!
CURLOCK: Oh! he looks through the papers and tells me What's-on! Joke, Watson, compris?
KAISER: Ah! Um! (*Pins Iron Cross on Watson.*)
CURLOCK: No wonder the Germans are running short of metal.
KAISER: You will obtain the dispatch, the paper? (*Pins another Cross on him.*)
CURLOCK: I must consult Dr. Watson.
KAISER: Ach! (*Pins two more Crosses on Watson.*)
CURLOCK (*taking Watson aside*): I'll accept the job, and when you show him out I want you to show him into the *safe* and turn the combination lock on him.
WATSON (*alarmed*): But we shall be blown to bits by Zep bombs!
CURLOCK: Not a bit of it, my dear Watson, I've sent them a wireless in the Kaiser's secret code telling them to call back later, as he's stopping the night.
KAISER (*impatiently*): Sauerkraut und Splitsodavasser! Vat is your answer?
CURLOCK: Most potty of Potentates, I am yours to command. By this time to-morrow the papers shall be yours.
KAISER: Zere Goot! Herr von Kurlock von Kombs. (*Pins three more Crosses on him and two on Watson.*)
CURLOCK (*striking a pose*): Imitation pin-cushion! Compris?
KAISER: To-morrow! If you fail the flaming sword of German Michael shall hew its way through you. (*Pins Crosses all over Curlock and Watson, and Watson shows him into the safe and turns the lock.*)
CURLOCK: Now he's safe, Watson. If his German Kultur can bite off a Chubb-Milner combination lock I'll, er, I'll join the Army. My suit case, Watson?
WATSON (*giving him suit case from under table*): Are you going out?
CURLOCK: Tell Madame we shall be back to dinner to-morrow. (*Rams a lot of absurd things into the bag, including an entrenching tool and several boxes of cigars, shuts the lid with the clothes protruding. Rams his hat on his head. Opens the door R and motions Watson to precede him. Stands at door and lights cigar.*) Ha! Ha! Let loose the dogs of war! The bloodhound on the scent. (*Sniffs.*) The British Bulldog never leaves go!

(*Poses for the curtain to fall, but it remains up while he keeps repeating "Never leaves go."*)

CURLOCK (*exasperated to scene-shifter*): Let it down, you fool!
VOICE FROM THE WINGS (*injuredly*): You said he never leaves go, didn't you!

CURTAIN.

ACTS II. AND III. *will appear in subsequent numbers.*

Abluting.

A CENSORED POEM.

There was once a time when water was as
    plentiful as dirt
  And a chap could keep his skin as white as
    snow,
He could even doff his tunic and his waistcoat
    and his ——
  But now he seldom sees un peu de l'eau
Excepting in the trenches, where his overcoat
    it drenches
  And tends his boots and tootsies to decay
It is certain to be muddy even if it isn't ——,
    And abluting in such liquid doesn't pay,
      anyway,
    Though you boil it up for drinking every
      day

In the days when every morning to the bath-
    room you would trot
  How you bragged about your early morning
    dip
In the icy, freezing water, though the tap was
    labelled ——
  And the cold one scarce contributed a drip.
But whether hot or chilly, now you'd use it
    willy nilly
  If only you could get it, never fear.
When your birthday suit you're dressed in, and
    your bath is just a ——
    You would even like to swim about in beer,
      but it's dear
    For it costs a franc a bottle over here.

But we get a bath just now and then when
    stopping in a town,
  We parade with soap and towel in the street
And you're wet for half a minute, so you very
    nearly ——
    Though the water doesn't cover both your
      feet :
Down your back it gently trickles and your
    (censorship) it tickles,
  And really the sensation's rather nice,
For you feel as bright and frisky as a seltzer in
    a whisky
    And you murmur that its cheap at half the
      price, kills the ——
    But the thing to do is—dodge, and have it
      twice.
          STROZZI.

♥ ♥

On Guard.

Ceaseless wail of a wind rain-laden,
  Gusts that sweep from bay to bay,
Blackness fraught with intensest horror,
  Powers of Hell let loose at play—
Anguish sore of a world in travail,
  Souls of men born noble, free,
Weltering now in a rout of carnage—
Why has this maelstrom sucked down me !

Twenty years have I passed in dreaming,
  Years that charmed with a mystic spell.
Why for me this rude awakening,
  Horror-surfeit ! Tell, O tell !
          BOW-WOW.

♥ ♥

Grand National.

SCENE.—A RESTAURANT.

Customer : I want some Turkey without
Greece.
  Waiter : Are you German
  Customer : No, I'm Hungary.
  Waiter : Then I can't Servia.
  Customer : Then it's no use for me to
Roumania.

♥ ♥

Common Sense.

Tommy (on active service) . Clean our
buttons ! why o' course we do !
  Inquirer (incredulous) : But what for !
  Tommy   Common sense ! Must 'ave clean
buttons every day—but clean shirts once in
three month's ! Like wearin' a shiny top 'at
and no boots, 'aint it ! Never mind, keep
smilin' !

IDEALISM.

"If only I could see dear George."   Dear George !!

WE know, but we shan't tell—

The name of the Corporal who murmurs in
his sleep, " Where's that other stripe ! "

Whether he has found it.

Who stood on the steps of the Divisional
Theatre and whistled for a taxi.

What regiment will in future be known as
the Royal Rifters.

Who said that Felix was h' un-eatable.

The name of the French scholar who said to
his billetrix, " J'ai venu dormer avec vous,
madame."

What the husband said !

Who are the grouse battalions.

Who received a tin of Maconochie as a
Christmas present from England.

♥ ♥

Rumour Hath it—

That zig-zags are not puzzles.

That the compiler of the German Official
Reports is to be asked to contribute to this
column.

That Ananias will accompany him as batman.

That we shall soon be given commissions.

That we shall never be given commissions.

That sappers are merely minor details.

That one of our cricketers will wear pads in
future.

That messie contacts are fond of moving.

Watch Night.

In England now the pious folk are passing
  Through darkened streets to watch the Old
    Year through,
Counting its good and evil, and amassing
  A stock of resolutions for the New—
The same in most part as they made the last
    And many years gone past,
    And kept them, maybe, for a week or two.

I doubt not each one reckons up the blunders
  That have prolonged (they've heard of it) the
    War
That one short year was to have won, and
  wonders
  If next New Year will find the business o'er—
If this year we shall shift the stubborn Hun
    And get him " on the run,"
    Or if he'll stick it for a couple more.

For us it's watchnight too. The sentry peering
  At No Man's Land across the parapet,
Shivers as, nothing seeing, nothing hearing,
  He thanks his lucky stars it isn't wet,
Till Fritz (a Sergeant probably—he's tight)
    Shatters the peaceful night,
    Licking all parsons that I've ever met.

He told us what they thought of us ; he wished
  us—
  Well, what he wished—for the approaching
    year ;
He told his comrades how, when they had
  dished us,
  The Fatherland should swim in Lager-Bier,
Stozzers, until we'd had enough
    And bade the blighter stuff
    His gas and lend instead his dirty ear.

You should have heard that chorus most
  derisive
  The " German Band," the Billingsgate so
    rare—
In fact we won a victory decisive,
  And Fritz could only list and tear his hair.
Then, vanquished in the warfare of abuse,
    The " Allyman " let loose
    His michiguns and strafed the empty air !
          TWOPENCE.

Printed and published for the Proprietors by WILLIAM
E. BARNETT, Journal Office, Castel, Salisbury.

A "Quiet" Day in Anzac Region.

By Corpl. J. Doggett, 15th Batt., Australian Imp. Force.

Between the offensive early in August, and the other big fights later on in this month, we had a few quiet days—quiet compared with the terrific activity of a determined advance, but whether these days merited the word quiet in its normal meaning I leave you to judge.

We were bivouacked well inland, not far from Hill 971. How that name is ineffaceably burned into the memory of all who took part in the attempts to capture and hold it during those awful days and nights of fighting.

There was no immediate likelihood of further attacks, for both the enemy and ourselves were busy consolidating our respective positions, and getting men and material sorted into some kind of order, after the bewildering battles in the hills and gullies.

This particular day I was one of a fatigue party detailed to bring up trench-digging tools from the beach. It meant a journey of about a couple of miles down to one of our supply bases by the seashore. Of course we paraded with our ammunition bandoliers and rifles, for wherever we went they came too; night and day we were inseparable.

When the Sergeant in charge had got necessary instructions, a start was made. We filed down our secluded gully, out on to a bit of cleared land. This showed signs of being lately cultivated, the yellow stubble being evidence of a saner occupation than that of killing men. Now we were visible to the enemy on the higher hills in the distance,

Told in the Huts.

and snipers' bullets were prone to come this way, so we spread out well, increased our pace, crossed the open space, filed along past a row of olive-trees, and again got under the shelter of a friendly hill. The Gallipoli sun was generous in its attentions, and our rate of travel slowed perceptibly.

Every now and then one of us would trip over some of our old field telephone wires, probably laid the first night that we marched out from Anzac. Wherever we advanced, close on our heels came the boys with their reels of copper wire, and so Headquarters kept continually in touch with its fighting Battalions.

We were interested to notice, as we walked, evidence of the departed Turks. There were gun-pits and positions everywhere, and we recalled how nearly these guns had come into our possession. But, alas! they had been dragged off just in the nick of time, and were destined to plague us again, sometimes seriously, sometimes otherwise. This same day we saw enough of the damage one gun can do, and if one of the enemy guns could discomfit us so, to what a tremendous extent our field and naval guns must have played havoc with them.

Discarded Turkish clothing lay about all along our road. One place in particular looked as though the Sultan's troops had cleared out in a panic, by the way garments and other stuff were strewn around. I think the Gurkhas had disturbed this particular bivouac, and if this was so, no need to wonder at the haste of "Abdul" in getting away, for Johnnie Gurkha has unique methods of his own.

Continuing our progress, we left the friendly cover of the hill, and got into a danger zone once again, and there we had ample evidence to prove that it were folly to linger, and we pushed on until we came under the lea of a small bluff, where one of our field ambulances had its tents pitched. Here we inquired as to the correctness of the report that the Turks were training their 75mm. French gun straight down

Electro-Contact Mine

A "Quiet" Day in Anzac Region.

the wide natural sap we had to traverse on our road to the beach. By the way, I might mention that this gun had been captured from one of the Balkan States during the war of a few years back, and we knew a little of the character of that type of artillery. It was hardly necessary for the A.M.C. men to advance any information, for close by were several wounded mules, and strewn about in an ominous way, cases of bully beef and other rations, all pointing plainly to the fact that our Indian Mule Transport had been caught by shells while coming up the roadway. This sap, as we called it, was no doubt the bed of a considerable stream in winter-time, but at that moment it appeared just a rough road track, sunken a few feet below the level of the adjacent country. There was this one stretch in front of us which the Turks could command with their artillery, and according to our informants they were using their 75mm. gun to harass this our communication road between supply base and fighting lines.

To march down in a crowd would court disaster with a vengeance; the best policy was to make a dash one at a time down this dangerous section. I don't suppose one of us felt fit to do a fairly long sprint, but one does a lot of remarkable things on active service.

While making this temporary halt at the field ambulance tents, along came a party of English Tommies. Their regiments were in position to the left of our lines, but their route to the beach was the one we were taking, and on this occasion their errand was of a similar nature to ours.

This was the first time I had had an opportunity of seeing together a number of Kitchener's men, who a few days before had landed at Suvla, so I was naturally interested in them. Poor chaps, they had experienced a rough time since landing, and, of course, the majority were new to the game. It was time to be moving, so off went the first of our boys. With rifle at the trail, away he went round the corner and down the exposed and deadly stretch. At short intervals others followed. Out would dash a six-foot Australian, then next, probably, a short, sturdy Tommy. Goodness! how they covered the ground. The shell of the 75mm. gives no warning like the scream of shrapnel does. It comes mysteriously, silent, and out of the immediate quietude there is just one abrupt nerve-racking report. No, none of us liked the 75mm.

It was my turn now. With a good grip of my rifle, I followed with a rush in the steps of the others, and in a second or so was racing down the deadly road. The track was strewn with awful sights. Not only did we have to dodge or jump over the mangled remains of pack mules, broken and splintered cases of various supplies, but there were human dead, some turbaned, others white-faced and khaki-clad. The artillery had done its work well. These poor remains were evidence enough. Their attitudes being so terribly pathetic and grim, one shrinks from penning a more detailed description.

So we raced on, dodging or leaping all obstacles, until, breathless, we one by one came round another friendly corner, where we could make a halt and recover ourselves. So far all was well, but we could not forget the same ordeal was to be overcome on our return.

Though we were now fairly secure from hostile shell-fire, we were still open to the attentions of the sniper, and surrounded by tragic reminders of his efficiency.

Now the sea came into view, but we had still some distance to go to get to our objective. What a thirst one cultivated on Gallipoli! Most of us had brought a little water in our bottles, and hoped to get more while down on the beach. After our sprint, of course, we had drank of our chocolate-coloured liquid supply rather recklessly, and before long our bottles were as dry as the Sahara, while our throat and tongue craved continually for more.

MIDST SHOT AND SHELL WE MADE THE NARROW BEACH.

A " Quiet " Day in Anzac Region.

One place we passed where an enemy machine-gun was sending a stream of bullets. It must have been firing at a great range. The ground where the bullets hit was quite a distance over from the track we had to follow. We watched these bits of lead kicking up the dust, and smiled at the way Abdul was so generously wasting his ammunition, for the bullets came high over our heads, and came to a stop farther on, right away from anybody or anything of value.

Some distance farther on we nearly had one casualty, for what was probably a sniper's shot just grazed the hand of one of our boys. He felt the momentary burn, but that was all, and though there were plenty of these bullets, bent on business, coming our way, by some marvel of fortune we did not stop even one of them. Now we got into a proper sap and were secure. At the other end we emerged out into a broad open space sheltered by hills at back, with the seashore in front. On this sandy stretch was the supply depot—our destination.

Our first action was to locate some place where we could refill our water-bottles. But though there were water-tanks handy, the crowd of men waiting their turn was so great, we felt like despairing of getting what we wanted from this quarter. Earlier that morning a hostile spy had been caught at these tanks; fortunately for us, perhaps, for in all probability he was there to tamper with the priceless water, and one could imagine the disastrous results had his mission been successful.

Our N.C.O. had located the tools we were to carry back, but we had to wait until the sun was less powerful before making the return journey. We foraged around for some dinner, and were successful in getting bully beef, biscuits, and some cheese. Our thirst was bad enough before this meal, but after the salt bully, and the dust and sun, it became chronic, yet still there was no hope at the water-tanks. By some happy chance one of our fellows discovered that

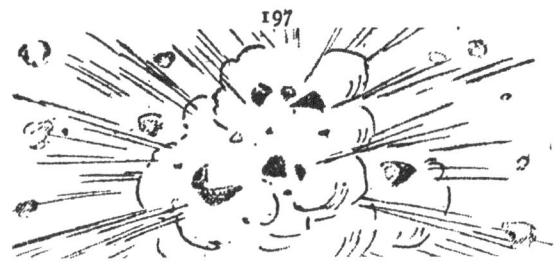

Told in the Huts.

a party of engineers were sinking a well right down on the beach. This place, about four hundred yards from where we were resting, was invisible to us on account of a rise in the ground. Those of us who heard of the chance to get water needed no urging to be off to try our luck, but to get to the well one had to cross an open belt of beach on which the enemy could fire. It was a case of another dash, only this time much shorter. A few bullets whizzed quite close enough, but a miss is as good as a mile.

We rushed over the roll or hump of ground, and I nearly tumbled over the bodies of half-buried mules. The stench from them was terrible, and I did not linger long. Soon we found the well, and with a little patience and strategy (for the engineers in charge had orders to conserve their limited supply for the time being), I had my bottle full and a good drink besides. If ever I enjoyed a drink it was this one, though it was only brown, gritty water, and the drinking vessel an old tobacco tin.

This little expedition over, I rejoined my mates, some of whom had taken shelter under canvas awnings. One or two chummed up to Indian mule drivers, and sat in the tents of the latter. Another of our boys, ignorant of the ways and customs of the Indians, made himself perfectly at home in the vacant tent of a Sikh who, apparently, was of a very exclusive caste. After a while the dusky warrior returned, and went into a fearful rage at the sight which met his gaze. I think the Indian thought the intruder had been drinking out of his private vessel, and in the eyes of the Oriental this was a great insult. Anyhow, he looked daggers at our now discomfited comrade, although the latter was really only guilty of using the tent as a good shelter from the sun.

Later came the word to bestir ourselves and prepare for the return trip. Soon we were all shouldering either a bundle of shovels or picks, and off we went again, heading

A "Quiet" Day in Anzac Region.

for our lines. The procedure was somewhat the same as when we came down, only our loads made progress slower. Just before we came to the area on which the 75mm. gun was ranged, we met a couple of Indians greatly concerned, carrying a third man who was wounded. The first glance told us he had not long to live, but how wonderfully considerate and tender were these two men to their comrade. Their actions were very inspiring. Next, we came to a wounded Tommy. He had received a bullet in the leg only a few minutes before, and word had been sent up to our field ambulance for a stretcher. We cheered the poor chap and continued. As we got into the danger zone of the 75mm., there came tearing down the road two of our stretcher-bearers. They were going to bring up the wounded Tommy. Once again I was struck with admiration for the boys of our Australian Medical Corps.

While we had been on the beach, the 75mm. gun had again been busy, and the road was a more terrible sight than when we had passed down earlier in the day. We hustled along as best we could with our loads, but what an age it seemed getting past this death-trap. Dame Fortune was kind though, and no shell burst over the roadway while we, stumbling and panting, zig-zagged our way round and over the still tragic objects that such a short time before had been live flesh and blood.

The sun had just hidden itself behind Imbros Island as we got back to our dug-outs on the gully side. The sunset was marvellous, sublime, but how could one enjoy even this great marvel of nature in such a war-stricken area as this? Other sights come to my mind—sights I had seen that day, though the happenings were only on a par with what was happening every day during a period which was termed and styled *quiet*.

Such is war.

True Till Death.

"YES," said my blue-clad companion, as he shook his head, "'True till Death' would be a suitable epitaph to place upon many a cross that marks the last resting-place of the heroes who have fallen abroad. All of them have not secured the Victoria Cross, but more lads have earned it than the few whose names are in the daily papers and who have been decorated by our King.

"I will tell you of one sight I saw, and the memory of it will always make me proud to be a Britisher—though a lump may rise in my throat as I recall the splendid heroism of that boy who was so true till death. He was only a lad, and the early years of his manhood had been spent behind the counter of a draper's shop in a small provincial town. But his yard measure was no index to the length he could go for the sake of his King and Country.

"He was a despatch runner—which is always a dangerous job to take on—and he worked between our lines and those of our gallant French allies who joined us upon our left. Our first line of trenches had been gassed by the Germans upon the previous night, and was then in their hands. The ground he had to cover was a death-trap to him each time he ventured out to carry his messages. What those despatches contained, none of us knew, but they did mean either victory or defeat to ourselves and our French comrades.

"I did not know the boy to speak to, though he was well-known to me by sight. I had watched him, three or four times a day, crawling up and down the near side of

True Till Death.

British Steel Helmets

the hedge that fringed the road between our lines. He was as game as they make them, with the instinct of a wild animal, and as reckless of danger as—well, as a Tommy.

"It was upon the third day after I had first noticed him, and early in the morning, that I saw him come creeping down towards us. He was upon his stomach, and nosing the ground like a setter. But I observed that, at quick intervals, he kept stopping and resting, with his face turned eagerly towards us, and his throat gasping for breath. The bullets were splashing up the mud all round him, as I had seen them do upon many a similar trip, but he only tightened the grip of his hand upon his side where the papers lay, and struggled a few feet nearer to us.

"It was then that the Turcos (the French colonial troops) were advancing across the near fields to reinforce us, and we were eagerly expecting the order to advance.

"But, before the boy could reach our trenches, he had to cross the road, where he lost the meagre shelter of the hedge, and was fully exposed to the open fire of the snipers. I could see that he was wounded, and that each movement of his body was an agony to him, but he struggled bravely on. I could almost hear his gasps as he reached the road. Then he stopped, and his hand fell limp against his side.

"His last word was a cry for help, for he knew that his time had come. But one of our lads was already on his way to the spot, and there was not a man who watched him but whose heart did not thrill with pride at knowing that he came of the same stock as those two grand men. The dying boy had only strength to feebly draw out his papers, and I could see the cruel red stain upon his hand. Then he kissed them as lovingly as a mother would kiss the babe at her breast, and gave them to his mate almost grudgingly.

"As he fell back into the mud, many an eye was dim at the sight, but a mighty cheer went up from our boys as the papers were brought safely into our trench.

Told in the Huts.

"I think it was the sight of those two glorious deeds that inspired us to do what followed. For the orders contained in that despatch were the very ones we were so anxiously longing for. We were to advance at once and storm the enemy's lines. Each one of us now felt that he had another crime to avenge—another deed of imperishable heroism to prove worthy of, for the sake of that boy who lay lifeless upon the road.

"The officer who led us fell dead within the first twenty yards, but, with a leader or without one, nothing could stop us then. We were like hungry, wild beasts set loose in a butcher's shop, and we not only took back the trench that had been lost to us, but we captured the German first line as well, and neither of them has gone out of our possession since that day.

"We left many of our poor lads dead behind us, but the figure that will always remain in my memory is that of the dying despatch runner, whose last breath was a kiss that brought us victory."

Trenching under Fire

The Philosophy of Swearing.

By E. G. Miles.

It was not a romantic spot by any means—not the sort of place where one would expect revelations. Like lots of other places to which reference is frequently made these days, it was somewhere in France, and like lots of other places in France it was crowded with British soldiers. The day had been cold and wet, everything and every place in camp was saturated, and as evening drew on, the Huts of recreation and entertainment quickly filled with crowds of men whose sense of homelessness drove them to shelter and company. The shelter was not perfect, but the company was as varied as the most hardened traveller could desire. Canadians, South Africans, Australians, New Zealanders, the Kilties and the Cockneys, rubbed shoulders together; the Welsh from London and the Irish from Lancashire exchanged views on the political situation. At the far end of the Hut was the counter; some men called it "the bar," and thereby gave away their attitude on the vexed question of teetotalism; others called it "the shop," at once revealing their mercantile origin; others, assuming the superiority of the Britisher who has explored the Continent, called it "the buffet"; but for purposes of description it must be called the counter, for it was a plain wooden structure standing three and a half feet high, and about as long as a cricket-pitch. The front of it was once covered with red distemper, but

Told in the Huts.

since those bright days it had been toned down to a greasy brown by the constant rubbing of clothes covered with trench mud. The top was covered with cork lino, and at intervals were steaming urns of tea and coffee, and barrels of ginger-beer and lemonade. Behind the counter were shelves laden with hundreds of buns and jam-rolls and packets of biscuits, and on the wooden partition at the back was a clock just striking eight. In the adjoining hall several hundred men were listening to a lecture, while in the canteen some were writing letters and others were looking at the pictures on the walls. These pictures were of as great variety as the soldiers. Most of the pictures were the artistic advertisements issued by British Railway Companies with the intention of alluring the fastidious holiday-maker of happier pre-war days. A discussion arose between some details of Northern and Southern Regiments on the respective merits of Blackpool and Brighton.

A crowd of men gathered round and joined in the give-and-take of opinion. It was not possible for all to join in the conversation, so from the fringe of the crowd some fell away. One big fellow came up to the counter, and blurted out, "Tea, jam-roll, packet o' fags." The jam-roll and packet o' fags were passed to him with amazing rapidity by the hands of a worker, who for three months had practised that art alone and was by this time proficient to the final degree. The tea followed—and being tendered by a more amateur hand, the mug caught on a protruding nail, and some of the hot tea spilled over on the man's hand. He mumbled something, and gripped tightly the handle, and looked me in the face with his lips closely pressed together and a savage glare in his eye. Before I could apologise for the little mishap, he said:

"If you wasn't a parson, I'd 'a swore, sir; I'd 'a swore a worse swear than you'd ever 'eard since Gawd made yer."

I was relieved, and at once replied:

The Philosophy of Swearing.

"Thank you for your restraint."

"For me what, sir?"

"For your restraint," I repeated. "I like to see a man control his temper, although I am to blame for spilling your tea."

"It wasn't temper, sir; it was 'abit, simply 'abit."

"I suppose you can't help it, sometimes," I ventured to say.

"Well, no, sir," he drawled on in a slow voice; "I don't think you can help it. It comes without an effort and it flows easy and natural, and somehow out here everybody understands the languidge; you see, sir, all the different parts of the British Empire understands it. In the Army the corporals understands it; the sargints understands it; the 'orses understands it, and the bloomin' motors understands it; and though I don't have anything to do with orficers, there's something inside me that tells me the orficers understands it too, the new orficers and the old. Everybody understands it. But I forgot for a minute that you ain't supposed to understand it. That's why I 'eld myself in, and I don't mind tellin' yer I'm quite proud of it; quite proud of it, I am."

As he finished, he stood upright and smacked himself on the chest.

"It must be a nice change for you to talk to someone who does not understand it," I remarked.

"Yes," he said, "you're right; it is a bit of a change, and I don't mind tellin' yer it's a bit of a strain to talk to a man as don't swear; at least as far as I know, you don't swear; yer see, it don't pay you to swear."

"What do you mean?" I asked, somewhat nettled at the insinuation.

"Well, what I means is simply this," he answered. "If you was to swear you would lose your job. I know you are paid not to swear; it's as clear as daylight why you

Told in the Huts.

don't swear. Now, if I gave up swearin', I'd lose my job. I'd be in the defaulters' compound if I didn't let off steam. Jist fancy bein' court-martialled for giving up a 'abit?"

"Are you treated so badly that you have to swear at everything and everybody and always?" I asked.

"Now then, sir, don't paint me blacker than I paint meself. Of course, I say a man must swear in the Army, or he would bust. But take me own case, I never swear at 'uman beings; I swear at objects, and I swear at wot you might call circumstances, and I swear at the silly things 'uman beings do; but I draw the line at a 'uman being."

"I do not see much difference between swearing at a human being and the things that human beings do," I replied.

"Oh, yes, there is," he said, "there's a very big difference. If I swears at my shovel, it don't do my shovel any 'arm, and it don't do me any 'arm; but if I swears at my pal Bill, it don't do Bill any good and it lets me down in Bill's estimation. Oh, no, I ain't one of those fools that swears at everything."

"But," I said, "you find enough to keep you going, don't you, in spite of your restriction against swearing at human beings?"

"Why, bless your 'eart, I should think so," he replied. "In this here war, there's enough things to swear at every day, to occupy every word of the languidge. I looks around me sometimes in the little dug-out and sees so many things in that little place to make a man swear, that I jist got to give it up in disgust."

As he spoke, the look of disgust seemed stamped upon his face. It occurred to me that this practised and discriminating blasphemer had not offered a specimen of his reserve powers since we started our conversation. I pointed this out to him, and took advantage of the occasion to notice that although the Hut was crowded and men in groups stood

The Philosophy of Swearing.

all around us, yet in the continued buzz of conversation there was not a single swear. The crowd was very representative, the men being browned with open-air; most of them belonged to fighting units.

The soldier listened attentively, like a poacher listening for game. After a minute he turned round, succumbing to the undeniable, and said:

"You're right, sir, quite right; there's no swearin' goin' on here; but all these chaps can swear."

"Well, they don't swear here, or at least I don't hear them," I replied, "and there are no notices forbidding it either."

"Quite right, sir. Quite right," he chipped in. "This is sort of out of bounds for swearin', and so it ought to be. I was listening to a man swearin' to-day, he was using up 'is words over and over again. I was thinking wot if a kind of big orficer came along with a pistol and stood over 'im and told 'im to go on swearin' and swearin', or he would put a bullet in him. He'd be shot right enough, 'cos there's a limit to swearin', and I believe that some of the chaps that go to hell will have to go on swearin' and swearin' till they are sheer wore out."

"That's a new idea of hell," I remarked. "What sort of a place do you think heaven is?"

"Well, now that you mention it," he answered, "I never thought about it till this very minute; but since you ask me, I don't mind giving you my opinion. It's a sort of place, I think, where nobody swears and where nobody wants to swear, and there ain't anything to swear about; why, lor' lumme, guvner, if you only knew how much swearin' some of us has got to do. It's awful, jist awful."

In the adjoining hall, where the lecturer had just finished his lecture, the men had gathered for family prayers, that beautiful custom which the Y.M.C.A. in France has

Hut Helpers

Told in the Huts.

done so much to encourage. The strains of a familiar hymn rose above the noise of the canteen—

"Heaven's morning breaks, and earth's vain shadows flee;
  In life, in death, O Lord, abide with me."

The men in the hall were standing for prayers, and the sound of united voices struck us when they prayed the Master's prayer, a moment's silence, and then the clatter of heels as they stood to attention for the National Anthem.

My soldier friend looked around at the crowded counters, the pictured walls, the rain-stained roof, the busy workers.

"I say," he said, "this ain't much of a place to look at; but nobody swears here, and nobody wants to swear here, and there's nothin' to swear about. It's a bit of all right, this is."

Tommy's Home

The Shell Hole.

OUR boys at the front may have grievances—reasonable and otherwise—with regard to the lives they live, but lack of excitement cannot be included among them. By day and night their hours are crowded with incidents, among which danger, pathos, sentiment, and heroic deeds play prominent parts. It is when we meet the now familiar blue-clad figures—often wandering along the deserted country lanes—that we wonder if the monotony of recovery from wounds is not harder to live through than was the tempest of shot and shell which left its badge of honour upon their maimed bodies.

In one of the fairest and most secluded of Sussex lanes the writer met one of these wounded men. He was a strapping young fellow in his early twenties, and his bandaged arm in its white sling bore eloquent testimony to the strenuous times through which he had passed not long ago. He shook his head thoughtfully when asked to recount some of his most thrilling experiences, and looked round at the peaceful scene as though it had no part in that other world of ceaseless noise and effort which he had left so far behind him.

"I should not know where to begin," he said, smiling shyly; "nor when to stop, if I did so; but they are living glorious times over yonder. Each day is a new-written page in the history of our Empire." He glanced down at his bandaged arm as he spoke. "I shall never regret that it happened, for I am more proud of this useless limb of mine than all the rest of my body. It shows I have done my bit

Told in the Huts.

for the homeland, and it is lucky I got off so cheap. My word! It was a nasty job while it lasted, and I was the only man out of three who came alive out of that hell of fire."

"Tell me about it. I should like to hear particulars of the incident."

For a few moments he was silent, as though reluctant to say anything which might appear to advertise his deeds of heroism. Then he straightened himself, and squared his shoulders, as though the smell of powder was again in his nostrils and the sound of bursting shrapnel in his ears— instead of the delicate perfume of autumn foliage and the carol of birds among the trees.

"I cannot tell the story well," he said, "though I can see the picture before me now in every detail. At times like that, there is always so much more that is felt than what is seen and heard. I suppose the principles of all warfare are immoral, but they were part of human nature long before there was any Church or State to define—and confine— the limits of morality."

This lad, in spite of having done his "bit"—or maybe because of it—was something of a philosopher.

"It was nearly midnight, and the rain had been coming down for days, so that the surface ground was a quagmire, and the trenches were knee-deep in water. There were three of us who climbed out over the sand-bags to reconnoitre 'No Man's Land'—and I was the only one who returned. There is no harm done in telling you the name of the place we started from, for there are plenty of spots out there in France and Belgium which will always be remembered as 'The Glory Hole.' We had literally to feel our way across the sludgy, rain-sodden mud, drawing ourselves slowly onward by gripping the tufts of grass and loose stones— with our eyes straining forward and with every nerve tight-strung. Each moment brought us nearer to the first line of the enemy trenches, and we did not know how many of

The Shell Hole.

the blighters might be prowling around us through that inky darkness. We must have crawled in this way about a couple of hundred yards, when suddenly the full moon came out from behind a bank of cloud, and the whole landscape was as bright as it is here now.

"You bet that we quickened our pace, for I do not think the moon ever shone as bright as she did at that moment, and the enemy snipers could have picked off a caterpillar from any of the tufts of grass in our hands. The only moderately safe refuge we could find was a Shell Hole —'Hell Holes' we called them—and they sprinkled 'No Man's Land' like the dents of a well-toasted crumpet. There we found the bodies of four dead Germans, and their appearance did not add one little bit to the comfort of our position. We could see they had been gassed by our boys, for their faces were black with pain, and the froth had got congealed upon their lips.

We only stayed there till the darkness was round us again, and we were right glad to leave that charnel-house behind us—for the Germans are horrible even in death. Our job was to get to the barbed wire in front of the first line of the enemy trenches, and report about the condition of it.

"It took us a long time to get there, but we reached it all right, and we found that the defences had been strengthened in a way we had not seen before. No man could have passed alive through them in the daylight with the bullets playing upon him. It was too dark for us to see the things, but we felt them all over carefully, and we then knew that our work had not been in vain.

"On turning to feel our way back to our trenches, we had not covered many feet when—to our dismay—we found that something had happened to the 'guide sticks' we had left behind us to show the direction we should take. Either they had been removed by enemy hands, or, what was more likely, the wind and rain had dislodged them in the slushy

Told in the Huts.

soil. The darkness was intense, and the danger of our position was made greater by the fact that without these 'guide sticks' our movements could only be made by guesswork. We had not advanced many yards when good luck brought us to a couple of the many Shell Holes around us. My mates got into one of them in double quick time, and I crawled into the other one. We only reached our shelter in the nick of time, for, as we did so, that old moon came out again to have a squint at us, and was brighter than ever.

"When I peeped over the edge of the crater, I saw that we were within thirty yards of the enemy's front line.

"Fortunately, our own men soon saw our cautious signals, showing that we were still alive, and the answer came back that we were to hold on where we were till the following night, if necessary. We were obliged to do this, and I think those hours were the longest in my life. I had no food from eleven o'clock—before I started on the trip—till seven o'clock upon the following evening. All the time I was hiding there the Germans were shelling our own front trench, and there was a regular duel going on from front to rear of me, with shrapnel bursting on all sides.

"The hole in which I crouched was about four yards from the one that hid my mates, and it was too risky to attempt any conversation. My arm was hit by a piece of shell early in the afternoon of that awful day, and, after that, I did not seem to care what happened to me. I was sick and faint with pain and hunger, and I thought each moment would be my last.

"I do not know when the terrible thing happened in the hole where my two companions were hiding, but I guessed they had been hit as soon as I saw they did not answer my signals. The agony of my wound had made me reckless long before it was dark enough for me to venture out into the open, but I knew that—if I was the only one of the three left alive—I should not take too great a risk.

The Shell Hole.

"So I waited as patiently as I could till darkness closed in again, and then I crawled over to that other shell hole.

"'How goes it, mates?' I whispered. 'Is there anything wrong? I have got a bit of a scratch myself.'

"There was no answer, and I repeated the question. Then I knew that the worst had happened.

"I got back to our front line all right, though I fainted twice on the way, and I just had enough sense left in me to report what had happened to my two pals and myself, and describe the new arrangement of wire defences ahead of us.

"Well, sir, those two brave lives were not given in vain, for our guns sent that blooming wire to blazes next morning, and a bombing party of thirty men attacked the German lines near which I had spent so many long hours. They left a good many corpses behind them, too, and brought back a tidy lot of prisoners."

Pinnace

Etiquette of Travelling.

THEY were in a crowded tramcar—a soldier almost helplessly drunk, my friend, and a very well-dressed man. A lady came in. The well-dressed man made no attempt to move—the soldier couldn't. My friend offered his seat. Looking across at the well-dressed man, the soldier said, "I'm drunk now and am a beast, but to-morrow I'll be a gentleman; you're a beast now, and you'll be a beast to-morrow."

Was it Superstition?

By Basil Yeaxlee.

THE draft had been in for about half an hour. From the Plain to the port of embarkation is not far as the crow flies, but the men felt as if they had been right round the British Isles, so long and tedious had the journey seemed. They had travelled through the night, and dawn had brought but a grey day. Partings were over, 'tis true, but not till the land is left behind, and the coast of France comes in sight, does the pang of farewell give place to the excitement and gay expectation of actually getting to the front at last. Moreover, some wore a gold stripe, or even two, upon their sleeves. They knew what faced them, though they were willing to face it over again, fifty times, if need be, rather than leave the job unfinished. So, while mouth-organs were in evidence, jokes circulating with perhaps rather more noise than usual, and rag-time the rule of the day, nobody wanted to linger over this last hour in "Blighty." But the tide didn't serve, and a couple of hours must pass before the boat could get away. The "rest-camp" was surrounded by barbed wire. Strolls in the town were beyond question. There remained the sign of the Red Triangle. Was there a Hut where the parting guests might speed themselves? Sure enough—and a particularly fine one.

Soon the long room was crowded with men, the bar was besieged by buyers of "Woodbines" and consumers of coffee. The air grew mellow with smoke; but the most striking part of the scene was the sudden fever of letter-writing that took universal possession of the battalion. Some—but they were few—scribbled a gay sentence on a picture post card. Others found a sheet too little for the sudden flow of ideas, and reached out for a second, and yet a third. Dozens

Was it Superstition?

Protected Scout

of men made a start, stopped, wrote a line or two more, reflected, tore up the paper, and tried again. A second, third, and even a fourth version alone sufficed for some.

One man got so far and gave it up. "Hang it!" said he to his chum. "Why can't I write? Never had any trouble in camp. Anyhow, it's of no use now. They'll have to wait till I get to the other side. Perhaps a few ideas will filter in then, and I may find an odd phrase or two without getting stuck. Come on, Dick, let's have a breath of air!"

Before he had managed to screw himself out of the crowd round the table, there resounded through the Hut a stentorian "Double up! Double up!"

"By jove, what a voice!" said the defeated letter-writer. "Fifty sergeant-major power. What?"

"Yes, and look at his chest," said Dick; "broad as Salisbury Plain. Three medals on it, too. And he's in mufti. Who is he, anyway, Jerry?"

"Oh, some Scot—listen to his a-a-ac-cent. What's that he's saying?"

It was a tale of three campaigns that was told from the platform—and there came, in a few shrewd, kindly, fatherly phrases, an appeal to these restless, eager lads, that they should be found,

"Through a whole campaign of the world's life and death,
Doing the King's work, all the dim day long."

*   *   *   *   *   *   *

After the intense quietness that filled the Hut while this brief but unforgettable summons was sounded, the babel that broke out seemed more overwhelming than ever. But there was a new look in many faces, and as the speaker moved among the boys whom he had been addressing, a hand was quietly shot out here and there, and a grip of gratitude given.

Told in the Huts.

Presently he took his stand by the door, at a little table covered with small books. As each man left he was accosted with a cheery demand, "Hae ye yir Testament noo, ma lad? Forgot it? Aye—of coorse. Did ye no forget yir razor, or d'ye no use one yet? Weel, here's another for ye—a bonnie, wee thin one for a corner of yir pooch."

Jerry paused and picked up one of the little thin-paper volumes. "Jolly good, guv'nor; I'll have one; but what are those? Oh, the same, only thicker. Well, give me one of the thick ones; perhaps it'll stop a Bosche bullet one of these days. You never know your luck. Besides, I'm a bit superstitious, you know. Well—don't take that last too seriously; I wouldn't distress you for worlds. Anyhow, this is going into my breast-pocket over my heart. And where shall I post this letter? Oh, there! Right O! You're a sport." He dropped his voice. "And, I say—er—thanks for that talk. I've just written a line home about it."

Apparently he had managed his letter after all.

* * * * * * *

The following appeared a few days ago in a certain famous West of England newspaper. Only names of persons and places are altered :—

"Miraculous escapes on the field of battle are not of infrequent occurrence, and it often happens that an article such as a book, cigarette-case, etc., deflects a shot that would have proved fatal otherwise. This has proved the case with Corporal I. F. D'Arcy, of the Loamshires, reported wounded in our columns of last week. He is lying at No. 3 General Hospital, and his most treasured possession is the little Testament issued by the Y.M.C.A. This has been cut to pieces by shrapnel the greater part of the way through, the Gospels being, with the first outside cover, intact. Protecting a vital part of the body, this unquestionably saved his life."

Three Boys in Khaki.

Cheero?

"MIND you, I do not say that any of the other fellows in our battalion would not have done the same, and be proud to do it," my companion said, "but those three jokers got the chance, and they took it. They deserve all the honour they got, and I hope they'll come back safe to 'Blighty' again, for I should like to grip their hands if ever we meet. They proved to me, what I had never doubted, and that is that when there is a pal's life to save, the British Tommy will run any risk, and does not care a tinker's cuss about himself.

"It was about four o'clock in the afternoon, and we were in the front line of trenches. The Germans were blazing away at us for all they were worth—and it looked as if they were worth a good deal too, when one of their shells burst just behind us, and blew old Joe right on to the top of the sand-bag parapet.

"Without a moment of hesitation, one of our lads—Private B., I will call him—rushed to rescue him, and, though he reached him all right, he was shot through the leg as soon as he had done so, and could not get back. But he took the wounded man in his arms, and sheltered him with his own body, making signs all the while for help to come, as he was unable to walk.

"He did not have to wait long, for directly they realised the predicament those boys were in, Sergeant —— and Corporal —— (I will not give their names) started to dig a small trench out to where they lay. It took some time to do, and they held their lives in their hands all the time, for they were under heavy fire, and what had been done once might be done again at any moment.

"It was a hard job, too, for they were working against time, and each moment that passed might easily have been

Told in the Huts.

the last one for the lot of them. I was watching them from my dug-out, and I can tell you that my heart was in my mouth when I saw that brave Sergeant shot straight in the middle of his right shoulder. But he set his teeth with an oath, and went on with the work quicker than ever, though every movement of his arm must have been a blinding torture to him. I saw the grim look upon his face, and it went as white as this sling. The great beads of sweat were pouring down his cheeks, making little trenches through the dust upon his skin.

" And, while those two men worked, I could hear Private B. upon the parapet. He was talking away with cheery words to the poor wounded fellow in his arms, and keeping him in good heart till the rescue party reached them. My word, but it was a fine sight, and one not easily forgotten! For the shells were bursting all round them, and they were digging away like mad for their stricken comrades, right in the very jaws of death itself.

" Each moment seemed to spin itself out into an hour: each foot of that slowly dug trench seemed to lengthen itself out into a mile: but still those two men stuck at the job, with never an upward look at the danger that was upon every side of them. I do not believe they even heard that hell of sound. One thought only was in both their minds: There were two wounded mates ahead of them, and they were going to be saved if hard work and good luck could do it.

" I suppose the whole incident was over in less than a quarter of an hour, and it seemed an eternity to me. They never spoke a word to each other, for they had no breath to waste, but I could hear the deep-drawn gusts of sound that came from their throats as they strained every nerve and sinew in a very frenzy of work.

" I could see that the Sergeant was getting faint with the pain of his wound, but he did not slacken his efforts for one moment. It seemed to give him a new strength that was

Three Boys in Khaki.

more than human, and inch by inch that trench gained in length till it reached the spot where the two wounded men were waiting. But, even then, the work was not finished, for sand-bags had to be fetched to make it secure from the German shell fire.

"It was then that Private B., with a deep gasp of relief, was first lifted down into safety. He had finished whispering his words of good cheer, for the fellow he had risked his life to save was already dead. Though his knee was shattered, he smiled bravely through his agony, as he tried to mutter his thanks to the rescuers.

"Together, and in silence, the Sergeant and the Corporal brought their burden back into their dug-out, and I saw them no more, for orders had been received to advance at once, and each man among us had about enough to do to look after himself.

"It was not till I got back here to old 'Blighty' again—and a bit of a wreck myself—that I read in the papers how those three brave lads had all been awarded the D.C.M. for what they did that day; and if ever men deserved to be honoured by their King and Country they were the fellows.

"It may not sound much, telling the story in this way, and sitting out here by the roadside with a 'Woodbine' between my lips. Only those who have been right up to the open doors of hell can guess the heroism of that deed. Those three men were the first to win distinction in our battalion, and I am proud to say that they were not the last.

"All the same, it is not taking away anything from their bravery when I repeat that I believe any two of the other boys among us would have done the same, and taken the same risk if they had been given the chance. Although I am only a Private myself, I can say, without conceit, that there is no man upon God's earth who can beat the British Tommy for pluck when there is a risky job to do, and Duty bids him do it."

The Sling Boys.

Sub: "What kind of a goat is this?"
"A 'Nanny' goat, sir."

The Optimist: "I am going to the concert to-night at the Y.M."

"Dear M——, I am sending you some money home—— But not this week, or the week after!"

Sketches by Bert Wardle, R.A.M.C.

Adding Insult to Injury.

"Perhaps I got more than I deserved when I was decorated with this 'ere Order of Merit," my companion said, as he pointed to an ugly, deep scar upon his right temple.

"How did it happen?" I asked, adding—with true civilian ignorance of military matters—"Was it a sword-thrust?"

Tommy gave a sniff of contempt.

"No," he replied, "it wasn't no sword, and it wasn't no billiard cue either. It was a blooming bomb that did it, and it was lucky it was such a rotten one."

I expressed surprise and interest at this piece of information. It was only politeness which made me refrain from suggesting that, if the head in question had not been so soft, the bomb might have exploded with still more disastrous effect. So I merely repeated my first question.

"How did it happen?"

"Well, it may sound rather a tall story, but I'll take my oath that it is as true as that I am standing here," was the reply. "It was when I was out with the Dardanelles Expedition that it happened, and at the time our first line of trenches was only twenty yards away from those of the enemy. My word! but we had a pretty rotten time of it out there. Never cool all day, and never warm at night. Our food consisted chiefly of bully-beef and bread, and each man was given one quart bottle of water per day for drinking and washing.

"We got fairly fed up with the life, I can tell you, so we used to amuse ourselves sometimes by trying to irritate those Turkish blighters whenever we thought they were near enough to hear what we said to them. Our favourite joke was to put our loaves upon the points of our bayonets, and hold them up for them to see—and envy. Then we shouted

Told in the Huts.

all together, 'Turkey finished,' just to give them a hint that we were living such a life of luxury, and that we had such an abundance of provisions and ammunition that they might as well chuck up the sponge at once, and do a 'Turkey trot' back to their old mosques and bazaars, and the rest of their tupenny peep-shows.

"One morning I had got a tin of bully in my hand, and the familiar sight of it nearly drove me off my nut. For, if it had not been for those bally Turks, and their bullet-headed cousins, the Bosches, I might have been at that moment back home in dear old Liverpool, and doing myself top-hole on a fourpenny dinner at Lockhart's. So I just took that tin, and I threw it for all I was worth right into the enemy's trench.

"'You can share it among you,' I shouted, 'and perhaps it will grease your joints a bit.' Then, as I could not speak their language, I added a little variety of my own, which they understand better in Liverpool than they do in the Dardanelles.

"It must have been a good shot, judging from the commotion it created. I heard a yell of fury, and whoever it was who was hit seemed to have a lot to say in expressing his thanks, though I did not hear him mention "Allah" once.

"I was standing with my back to the blighters at the time, when one of our boys shouted out to me to 'look out.' I was just going to follow his advice, when a bomb came whizzing against the side of my head, cutting my skin to the scalp bone.

"It was a dirty trick to play, especially after my offer of friendly hospitality. But what hurt my feelings far more than the thing which hurt my head was the fact that, when we picked up that rotten bomb and examined it, we found it had been made in Scotland.

"And my mother came from Aberdeen."

Y.M.C.A. Men who have Won the V.C.

By Basil Yeaxlee.

Many thousands of Association men have joined the Forces during the War. Hundreds have laid down their lives on Active Service. Distinctions have been won by brave deeds and fine comradeship. The V.C. has been awarded to a number of Y.M.C.A. members, and the present volume would not be complete without a brief account, as far as information is available, of the achievements that won them the Cross.

Lance-Corporal Leonard James Keyworth, V.C.,

of the 24th County of London Battalion, was long known in Lincoln as a good sportsman. A keen footballer, he was also a valuable "left-hander" in the Y.M.C.A. cricket team. Captain F. B. Galer, Adjutant of the 3rd Battalion, who enlisted him, says: "I well remember him as one of the pick of the finest Territorials you could wish to see." The Germans will doubtless cherish similar recollections of him, for during the British attack on Givenchy trenches, fifty-eight out of seventy-five men from his battalion were killed or wounded, but he stood fully exposed on the top of the enemy's parapet and threw about 150 bombs among the Germans, who were only a few yards away. Like Sergeant O'Leary, he thought this quite the obvious thing to do, and after being recommended for special mention, wrote: "It is supposed to be for bravery, but I cannot understand where it came in, as I only did my duty. But how I came out God only knows."

Firing Rifle Grenade

Told in the Huts.

He heard that he was recommended for the Distinguished Conduct Medal, but found a fortnight later that he had been awarded the V.C. Officially, this was in recognition of his exploit as a bomb-thrower. As a matter of fact, he had also made a chivalrous attempt, at great risk to himself, to save a wounded Lieutenant that same night, and his mother received a letter from the Lieutenant's mother, adding this to the story of his bravery.

Like so many others who have won the supreme military distinction, he returned to the Front, after having been fêted in his native city, to face again the ardours and perils of Active Service, only to fall in the fight.

Temp. Sec.-Lieut. Donald Simpson Bell, V.C.

The following is the official story of another who crowned his winning of the Cross by rendering the great sacrifice:

"Temp. Second-Lieutenant Donald Simpson Bell, late Yorkshire Regt., for most conspicuous bravery. During an attack a very heavy enfilade fire was opened on the attacking company by a hostile machine-gun. Second-Lieutenant Bell immediately, and on his own initiative, crept up a communication trench, and then, followed by Corporal Colwill and Private Batey, rushed across the open under very heavy fire and attacked the machine-gun, shooting the firer with his revolver, and destroying the gun and personnel with bombs. This very brave act saved many lives, and ensured the success of the attack. Five days later this gallant officer lost his life performing a very similar act of bravery."

The Secretary of the Harrogate Association writes: "D. S. Bell was an old member here, and one of the most popular ones; he represented Yorkshire in the International Y.M.C.A. Football Team that toured Denmark three winters ago."

Y.M.C.A. Men who have Won the V.C.

Private Edward Barber, V.C.,

Grenadier Guards, aged twenty-two, a member of the Tring Y.M.C.A., was awarded the V.C. for bravery at Neuve Chapelle. He ran in front of a grenade company, and threw bombs with such effect that numbers of the Germans at once surrendered. When his company came up, Barber was found quite alone with the enemy surrendering all round him. He was afterwards killed by a sniper's bullet.

Sergeant Claude Castleton, V.C.,

late of the Australian Contingent, joined the Lowestoft Association in September, 1910, and was a member for two years up to the time of his leaving this country to seek a larger life in Australia. He is remembered by many of the present members as a keen gymnast and a strong, manly, open-air fellow. The record of his devotion, contained in a letter from one of his comrades, fully bears out their knowledge of his bravery and resolution of character.

"We were helping to hold a first line of trenches, when our infantrymen made an attack on the enemy. As may be expected, we had some casualties. Claude, knowing some of our wounded men to be out in 'No Man's Land,' could not resist going to their assistance. Amidst shrapnel and heavy machine-gun fire, rifle-fire, and gas, he leaped out, had rescued two wounded men, and was in the act of bringing in the third, when, to our sorrow, he was hit by either rifle or machine-gun fire. First-aid men went to his assistance immediately, but could do no good. He had done his last. We gave him a decent burial behind our front line, erecting a small cross with his name, number, etc., over his grave. His name will stand for ever amongst the officers and men of his company, and also with the infantrymen and officers to whom we were attached. His name is being mentioned by all, for not only is it on this occasion that we have found

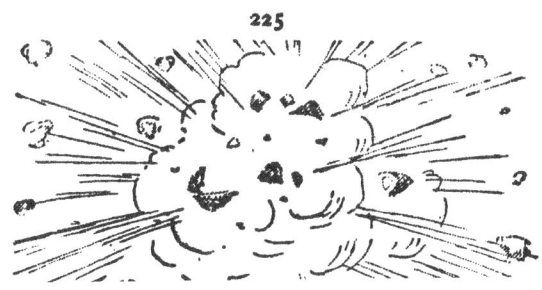

Told in the Huts.

him a leader, but at Gallipoli, after losing an officer and sergeant, we looked to Claude as our leader, and from then up to the time of his death we were ready to follow him anywhere, having confidence in him as a leader of true British spirit, and we know how difficult it will be for a man of his ability to be replaced." He was awarded the Victoria Cross.

Corporal James L. Dawson, V.C.

The Victoria Cross was awarded to Corporal James L. Dawson, a former Alloa Y.M.C.A. member, for conspicuous bravery. A supplement to the *London Gazette* gave, amidst the particulars of deeds that had won the Cross, the following account of his achievement :

"No. 91608, Corporal J. L. Dawson, 187th Co. Royal Engineers, for most conspicuous bravery and devotion to duty on October 13th, 1915, at Hohenzollern Redoubt. During a gas attack, when the trenches were full of men, he walked backwards and forwards along the parades, fully exposed to a very heavy fire, in order to be better able to give directions to his own sappers, and to clear the infantry out of the sections of the trench that were full of gas. Finding three leaking cylinders, he rolled them some sixteen yards away from the trench again, under very heavy fire, and then fired rifle bullets into them to let the gas escape. There is no doubt that the cool gallantry of Corporal Dawson on this occasion saved many men from being gassed."

Corporal (Acting Sergeant-Major) Dawson is a native of Tillicoultry, was educated at Alloa, graduated M.A. at Glasgow University, and was, until enlistment in October, 1914, Science Master in a Govan School.

Corporal James D. Pollock, V.C.,

a member of the Paris Y.M.C.A. (Anglo-American Branch): "On September 27th last, when the enemy's bombers in superior numbers were successfully working up the Little

Y.M.C.A. Men who have Won the V.C.

Willie trench towards the Hohenzollern Redoubt, Corporal Pollock, after obtaining permission, got out of the trench alone, walked along the top edge with the utmost coolness and disregard of danger, and compelled the enemy's bombers to retire by bombing them from above. He was under heavy machine-gun fire the whole time, but continued to hold up the progress of the Germans for an hour, when he was at length wounded."

Corporal Pollock has recently been granted a commission in the gallant Camerons.

Doubtless many more Y.M.C.A. men will win the Victoria Cross before the war is over. They will therein prove their loyalty to the motto written on the wall of every Red Triangle Hut in the world: "For God! For King! and for Country!"

A Question of Gender.

THE Belgian soldier turned to the lady whom he had been questioning, and with native courtesy said, "I am afraid, madam, that I cockroach upon your time." She, wishing to set him at ease, and at the same time to correct his mistake, replied, "Here we say 'encroach.'" "Ah," said the Belgian, "for you, madam, it is right to say 'hencroach,' but for me it is proper to say 'cock-roach.'"

The "Scotch" lady who had been an interested listener, afterwards remarked, "Isn't it strange how some people will always put the aspirate in the wrong place?"

The Prodigal.

"SPEAK to that man, yonder," said one of the ladies; "he is over on leave, but says that he does not intend to go home."

After a while we chatted and made friends. He said that it was eight years since he left England, having gone straight to the Front from India.

"Of course, you are going home?" I remarked.

"No! I am going to spend my leave in London."

"Perhaps you have no people?"

"Oh, yes! Mother and father."

"And not going to see them! How is that? Did you quarrel?"

"Yes, sir."

"But surely you'll see them before going back? You may never have the chance again, and it would be cruel to return to the Front and deny them the opportunity of seeing their boy again. Won't you go?"

"I'm afraid, sir, I haven't time. I have wasted half my leave."

"Well, do you mind my looking at the time-table to see just how much time you would have?"

"All right."

"If you leave at such a time, you'll have exactly forty-eight hours at home. Will you go?"

With tears in his eyes he said:

"Yes!"

"Will you wire to them now to say that you are coming?"

"All right."

My last memory of him is a hearty hand-grip and a hurried farewell as his train steamed out of the station "homeward-bound."

French Mountain Gun

"The Wowser."

HE had just booked his bed, and with his head and the greater part of his body thrust through the office window, he waxed reminiscent.

"At the time I joined the North Auckland Mounted Rifles, another man, tall and weedy-looking (Dai Williams by name), tried to join, but was turned down, being physically unfit. He happened to be a theological student and a Y.M.C.A. man, so had a shot for a Chaplaincy, but still without success. Having means of his own, and being determined to join up somehow or other, he paid his passage to Egypt, and ultimately became attached to our unit.

"While we were in Cairo he constituted himself a sort of guardian angel to the men of our battalion. Many a time he would be seen strolling into one or another of the dens of infamy in the Waya quarter and fetching out, most unceremoniously, any of ours whom he might find. Physically inferior to any one of us, he had a compelling manner, a magnetic personality that none of us could resist. How we hated and despised him—called him 'The Wowser,' and many like terms—but he persisted.

"Later, when we moved to Gallipoli, he went with us. He would fetch and carry for any of us; many a helping of food and drink was brought to us in the front-line trench by him, and sometimes a weary man on sentry-go would suddenly discover 'The Wowser' beside him, still fulfilling his self-appointed rôle of guardian angel.

"There came a day when we dashed from our trenches across to the enemy lines. Somehow or other 'The Wowser' got mixed up with us, and when officers had fallen, actually

The Optimist

Told in the Huts.

led the charge. By this time our feelings towards him had so changed that any one of us would have willingly given our own life rather than he should be hurt, but he stopped a few bullets, and came down badly wounded. I think he still lives, but whether or no, he was a man, a true Christian, a d—— hero."

[*The foregoing is given pretty much as told, although shorn of much of its adjectival language.*]

The Wanderer from Clare.

THE taller of the two gunners introduced himself and friend to me as "the man from Galway," and, said he, pointing to his friend, a clean-shaven, red-headed, sturdy, thick-set man with a face full of good humour and fun—"the Wanderer."

The "Wanderer from Clare" informed me that he was just going on leave, but that he thought another two months after his return would see the finish of the war.

They were very talkative, and could with difficulty be induced to go to bed. At last they agreed, but said they must have a last drink. It was set before them, and "The Wanderer," leaning forward, said in his best Irish manner, "Can't you put a drop of something in it?" Reaching down a bottle of O.T., I proceeded to oblige. "The Wanderer," noticing this, half-emptied his glass to leave more room for the "drop." I obliged his friend also, and was placing his glass before him, when "The Wanderer" held my hand and said, "No! Let me drink it first, to see how he likes it." He drank his own, and in a gasping voice, and tears in his eyes—for the "drop" was of decided strength—he said, "Yes, sorr; he likes it."

A Forage Wagon

"Smuggy."

WE called him "Smuggy" in the old days, when he was just a kid in our village at home, because he always carried such a smug, well-satisfied smile upon his face. It was a smile that got upon our nerves, for it was a sort of laugh half-cock, and we other lads put it down to swank. He was not a popular boy either, for he kept a good deal to himself, and he never joined in our games. Most of his time was spent in collecting bugs and beetles, and there was an article by him about tadpoles in the County *Courier* before he was sixteen years old.

But that is all ancient history now, and it does not come into this yarn. I was working on my father's farm, and "Smuggy" was serving in the village shop, when the great war started in 1914, and we were the first lads in the district to join up. I do not know if it was by accident or intention, but "Smuggy" and I both found ourselves in the same regiment, and I suppose they were the old home ties that made us chum up together in our new life in a way that I should never have thought possible in the old days.

I daresay I could fill a book with the adventures we shared and the sights we saw when our boys were ordered to the Front. But I would like to tell of one experience I had; not because of the part I played in it, but because, if it had not been for "Smuggy," I should not be here now, but under a wooden cross "somewhere in France."

It was my first and only experience of taking part in a bombing raid. There were eight or ten of us—one of whom was "Smuggy"—and we started upon our expedition at eleven

Told in the Huts.

o'clock one dark, rainy night. We looked a queer lot, I can tell you, as we crawled out of the advance post, for our faces and hands were blackened with soot from the cookhouse, and we all wore clothes that had been taken from German prisoners, so as to make identification as difficult as possible for the enemy. Each one of us also carried a small white patch upon his tunic, so that our own sentries might know we were English boys when they challenged us. The usual orders were left behind, that there was to be no firing from our trenches till we returned from "No Man's Land." Besides the actual bombers, our party also consisted of bayonet men and wire-cutters. As the enemy were constantly sending up their white rockets, we had particular instructions to remain in whatever positions we were in when they did so. We were not even to wink an eyelid if we could help it, and Heaven help us if we wanted to sneeze.

Our officer was leading us, and he was followed by the wire-cutters. Then came the bomb-throwers, and last of all came the bayonet men, whose business it was to deal with any of the enemy who had not already been killed. Few prisoners were ever taken during these expeditions, and they were only for the purpose of obtaining information, either verbally or from papers found upon them.

We got to the wire entanglements all right, and then our work began in real, grim earnest. At the explosion of the first bomb, the night seemed suddenly to burst into a regular fury of sound and movement. Yells of pain and fierce guttural oaths came from every side of us, and we simply fought like mad dogs. I had the worst luck of any man in our party, for I was soon wounded in the throat, and got a broken shoulder. But I did not mind that so much, for I knew I had accounted for three Bosches. I remember I felt no sensation of fear nor of pain at the time—only a red fever of excitement which made me absolutely

Bomb throwing

"Smuggy."

reckless, and gave me a strength which I have never possessed before nor since.

As soon as our supply of bombs was exhausted, the order was given to retire. They and the bayonets had done their ghastly work well, and we stumbled over many corpses as we made our way back to the spot from which we had first entered the trench.

I was the last one of the party to reach the parapet, but, as soon as I knew that my job was over, a horrible reaction set in, and I do not mind owning to it. I trembled like a leaf. I do not think it was due so much to the horror of what I had seen and done, as to the ghastly pain of my wounds. One of my arms was useless, and the gnawing agony of my throat made me feel sick and faint. I could just lift myself very slowly up to the ledge above me, and, as I did so, I knew I was standing upon the body of a man.

Observation Kite

I paused, to ease my position a bit, and at that moment I felt a hand feebly grip my foot—and hold it.

For the life of me I could not free myself, and the gash in my neck made it impossible for me even to whisper to the next man ahead of me. Weakly as those fingers clutched my ankle, I felt that they were pulling me backwards—back again into that horrible place of darkness, where men lay dead and dying—where the unseen ground was red and slimy with warm human blood.

I tried to shriek out to my mates, but the effort to do so only made the pain worse than it was before. My left hand was clutching a tuft of grass, and, as it yielded to the pressure, I sank slowly and noiselessly down upon the man whom I knew was waiting to take my life.

Though he might already be in the throes of death, I was helpless and in his power. The only thought in my mind at that moment was the question—"Is he strong enough to kill me, or will he die first?" I felt the touch of fingers moving gently up my leg till they reached my waist.

Told in the Huts.

My left hand closed upon them, but could not stop their progress. Instinctively I guessed that he was feeling for my throat. If once those bloody hands reached my wound, he would find that his work was already half done. The hand moved, toad-like, upwards upon my chest, and, as it touched my bare skin, I lost consciousness.

How long I lay there in that condition I do not know, but the next thing I remember was hearing the sound of a low voice whispering into my ear, and all the pain seemed to leave my body as I recognised that it was "Smuggy" who was speaking.

"For God's sake, let me get you out of this place before it is too late," I heard him say. "Can you pull yourself together a bit, lad, or shall I lift you?"

I could not speak, but I found his hand and pressed it gently, just to let him know that I was alive.

Well, I am not a little fellow, and "Smuggy" certainly was not a Hercules, but he managed to get me out of that death-bed, and he did so as tenderly as possible. Then he carried me back to our own trenches, with never a backward look at the horror we were leaving behind us.

"I missed you, my boy," he said, "when we were half-way upon our return journey, so I went to find you." He gave a short grunt of satisfaction as he spoke. "I think I was only just in time to spike that Bosche, though, before he did for you. My word! But he would have made a beautiful beetle!"

I have not seen "Smuggy" since that night, but I have told this story many a time in our village at home, to the old folk there, who always did say that there was more in the lad than we gave him credit for in the old days, in spite of his smile and his swank.

"Be British—Keep Off."

EARLY in the War H.M.S. *Formidable* was torpedoed in the Channel. In the dead of night an enemy submarine crept within range and lodged two deadly torpedoes, which sunk the battleship. There was no panic, and, face to face with death, officers and men alike worthily upheld the best traditions of the British race.

Standing on the bridge, giving instructions as coolly as if he were merely on manœuvres, the Captain made his appeal to the men: "Keep cool, don't vex the nation"; "Be British, don't vex the nation." Then, as other boats prepared to come to the aid of the *Formidable*, he signalled them to "Keep off." He remembered the fate of the *Cressy* and her sister cruisers, and feared that, in trying to rescue him, the boats that were coming to his aid might share the same fate.

It is great to be British in the face of danger, disaster and death, as were the men of the *Formidable*. Amongst the number was a young Middy. He heard the Captain's appeal to be British, and no one could have responded to the challenge better than he did. When the men were paraded on the deck, he knelt in prayer before them all. His prayer finished, he rose to his feet and saluted the flag, and went down with the ship. There is not much the matter with dear Old England whilst she has sons like these, and, thank God, there are many. Every day the public press tells the story of undying heroism, and Mr. Lloyd George may well say, in speaking of the heroism of our men, "We thought these qualities were the qualities of the great, the choice and the select. They are all great, they are all select. The War has turned out a nation of heroes."

A. K. Y.

Battleship.

The Story of an Ambuscade.

DURING those first terrible months of the War, a company of Yorkshire troops had been told to occupy a village in Northern France, and their scouts had informed them that it was clear of the enemy. With swinging steps they entered the one long street of which the village consisted, singing an English chorus with great gusto, and in the very best of spirits. They had hardly entered the village when, at the other end of its one long straight street, they saw a lad in khaki jump out from the front door of a house on one side, and spring into the middle of the street. The rifles rang out, and they saw the lad fall dead. Running forward as quickly as possible, they found the young soldier dead, with no fewer than eleven German bullets buried in his body. They ascertained afterwards that in some way or another he had been taken prisoner by the Germans the previous night. They thought they were perfectly safe in letting him wander at will through the house. He knew, and they knew, that if he attempted to give warning he would be a dead man. They were lying in ambush for his comrades—the Yorkshire troops—information of whose movements had been given them by their spies. When the moment came, without hesitation, he sprang out to give warning, though he knew it meant certain death.

They never ascertained his name—even the identification disc was missing, and there was no method of identifying him. In the morning he was buried in a nameless grave, and over it his comrades placed a rough cross of wood, on which was written:

"He saved others. Himself he could not save."

A. K. Y.

Printed by Jarrold & Sons, Ltd., Norwich, England.

Cheero?

CPSIA information can be obtained at www.ICGtesting.com
Printed in the USA
BVOW10s1053240614

357222BV00005B/258/A